starred in the original 1970s
aptain Ross Poldark. It is widely
lar British costume dramas ever
produced, beloved in more than forty countries around the world.
Robin returned to television to play a cameo in the new twenty-first-
century adaptation of the series, produced by Mammoth Screen
on behalf of the BBC and PBS/Masterpiece – enchanting a new
generation of TV viewers.

Other TV and film appearances have included roles in *Fawlty Towers*,
Elizabeth R, *Blue Remembered Hills*, *The Good Soldier*, *The Europeans*
and *Heartbeat*. He had a long and successful career in British theatre
too, including a stint with the Royal Shakespeare Company.

In 1999, Robin was diagnosed with Type 2 diabetes. Although he
had no symptoms, he took the diagnosis seriously as his mother had
suffered with Type 1 diabetes for thirty-five years. In the same year,
he and his wife, Meredith, moved to southwest France, where he has
become known locally as the 'Anglais who cooks'! By changing the way
he ate and taking more exercise, Robin was able to control his blood
sugar sufficiently to avoid taking medication for six years. Inspired by
a lifelong passion for cooking, he wrote his first cookbook, *Delicious
Dishes for Diabetics: A Mediterranean Way of Eating*, in 2011. His second
cookbook, *Healthy Eating for Life: Over 100 Simple and Tasty Recipes*
(2014), is aimed at everyone wanting to eat more healthily without
sacrificing good taste. His memoir, *Making Poldark* (2015), also
touches upon the positive effect his diagnosis ultimately had on
his lifestyle.

Robin blogs regularly on food, cooking and life in rural France
at http://robin-ellis.net. He also leads popular healthy cooking
workshops in Lautrec, France, famous for its pink garlic festival.

In this wonderful recipe collection Robin shares his favourite dishes
so that other Type 2 diabetics and their families can enjoy the benefits
of a healthy Mediterranean style of cooking.

There's an old Basque saying:

'To know how to eat is to know enough.'

Mediterranean Cooking
for Diabetics

ROBIN ELLIS

ROBINSON

First published in Great Britain in 2016
by Robinson

Copyright © Robin Ellis, 2016
Photography by Meredith Wheeler

1 3 5 7 9 10 8 6 4 2

Important Note
The recommendations in this book
are solely intended as education and
information and should not be taken as
medical advice.

A CIP catalogue record for this book
is available from the British Library.

ISBN: 978-1-47213-637-4 (trade
paperback)
ISBN: 978-1-47213-638-1 (ebook)

Designed by Andrew Barron
Typeset in Whitman and Scala Sans
Printed and bound in China

Robinson
is an imprint of
Little, Brown Book Group
Carmelite House
50 Victoria Embankment
London EC4Y 0DZ

An Hachette UK Company
www.hachette.co.uk

www.littlebrown.co.uk

Michael Pennington, actor and author:

'Robin Ellis has the gift of writing recipes that you can taste as you read them. As if his acting weren't enough, he's now given us a marvellous book – without any pretension or carry-on, just deep affection and knowledge. Absolutely delicious.'

Eva Marie Saint, Hollywood legend, Academy-Award and Emmy winner:

'Robin Ellis is a superb chef! His cookbook is filled with delicious and healthy recipes even for people like me who are not diabetics.'

Tim Pigott-Smith, actor:

'It is always a joy to visit Le Presbytère. It is the most beautiful house, which reflects the calm of its isolated position and the nearby chapel. At the centre of this old building – whose thick walls guarantee that you can find relative cool even on the hottest day – is the small crowded kitchen.

'The sight of Robin – fully aproned, glasses strung round his neck, peacefully looking for spices, strolling out into the courtyard for a fresh fig to enliven a salad, or hunched over a saucepan stirring a fortifying soup – is surprising for anyone who remembers him striding across the stage at Stratford, or riding round Cornwall.

'However, it is here where he has truly found himself, in this house and in this room. As my wife Pam and I have been privileged to do many times, you can now enjoy its proceeds.'

Imelda Staunton, actress:

'How can food this good be this good for you!'

Timberlake Wertenbaker, playwright (Our Country's Good):

'I've used Robin's recipes again and again. They're elegant, delicious, imaginative and easy to use.

'The Basques are great cooks and giving a dinner in the Basque Country is scary. One also eats very late, so no one wants anything too heavy. I always use one of Robin's recipes and end up with nothing but compliments and a demand for the recipe.

'"An Englishwoman who can cook tuna!" someone said to me in complete astonishment. Of course, the recipe was Robin's.'

Also by Robin Ellis

Delicious Dishes for Diabetics: A Mediterranean Way of Eating

Healthy Eating for Life: Over 100 Simple and Tasty Recipes

Other cookery titles from Robinson

A Lebanese Feast

Delicious Gluten-Free Baking

Everyday Lebanese Cooking

Patisserie

The Healthy Slow Cooker Cookbook

Contents

Appreciations

The success of my first cook book,

Delicious Dishes for Diabetics, helped to persuade Nikki Read and Giles Lewis of How To Books to build on the idea of an accessible book of Mediterranean recipes aimed at people with diabetes – or trying to avoid it. They saw the value of a book promoting healthy eating without the prospect of a life sentence of culinary deprivation and sacrifice. I have enjoyed our partnership and am grateful for the confidence they have shown in the project.

And thanks to Judith Mitchell, who edited my first two books and without whose guidance and faith we wouldn't be here now.

Thanks too to Duncan Proudfoot, Publishing Director at Robinson for his contribution. He was present back at the launch of my first cookbook and I'll never forget his kind words of support.

My gratitude also to the team at Robinson/Little, Brown, including Amanda Keats, who have worked so patiently to get the details in the text and in the recipes right and making sense!

I also wish to thank the dear friends who have dined with us around our kitchen table and been so generous in their endorsements.

My original cookbooks were enhanced by the beautiful, atmospheric drawings of our friend, Hope James. This new book, with its larger format, has expanded into the world of photography. Meredith Wheeler, my wife, has been taking pictures of the food I cook for years and it seems natural that these wonderful photos, along with other incidental shots of life here should illustrate the book.

Thank you, Meredith, for your willingness to delay tasting the first mouthful until you have 'got the shot'!

'A table tout le monde!'

Introduction

This book is written for people who love food, enjoy cooking and wish to continue those pleasures despite a diagnosis of Type 2 diabetes. It is also for those people who love them – because the Mediterranean way of eating is healthy for everyone.

In terms of food, though I live in France, my heart is in Italy. (It's all to do with fresh ingredients prepared simply.) One of my favourite places to eat in Florence is Mario's – a small family-run café near the wonderful St Lorenzo food market. It's a modest place – only open for lunch – but always packed with marketers and those in the know. Complete strangers are wedged together at the same tiny table. Last visit, I ordered their grilled veal chop with herbs and a plate of white beans with olive oil. Simple – yet sublime! That is how I like to eat and to cook.

This is an anthology of recipes I have collected over the years, recipes I have found reliable and easy to follow – not fussy or difficult. The dishes have a Mediterranean flavour – favouring olive oil, garlic and tomatoes as basic ingredients.

It's not a diet cookbook; rather it's a 'way of eating and cooking' book. There *is* something temporary implied about following a diet, rather like 'taking the medicine' – it'll be over soon and one can get back to normal life. The way of eating in this book *is* normal life!

Shortly after I was diagnosed with Type 2 diabetes, a friend recommended Michel Montignac's book, *Dine Out and Lose Weight*, now re-titled *Eat Yourself Slim… and Stay Slim!* I found it helpful. He too emphasised the importance of changing one's 'way of eating' rather than dieting.

Montignac was from southwest France, where a culture of eating well is central to a good life. One of the attractions of his eating plan is that it allows you to drink wine (in moderation) and to eat a couple of small squares of high cacao dark chocolate. Oh, happy days!

As a young man, Montignac struggled with his weight. After working as a manager in the pharmaceutical industry, he left to research and develop his theory of why people put on weight and to find a way to prevent it. He believed that it is the high sugar content in some carbohydrate foods that encourages the body to store unwanted fat, rather than a high calorie intake. He was a pioneer in using the glycaemic index (GI) of foods (see page 220 for further explanation), which measures the effect of carbohydrates on blood-sugar levels (how quickly carbohydrates turn to glucose in the blood) to help people lose weight.

Controlling one's weight is a primary concern for people with diabetes.

I had witnessed my mother's long struggle with Type 1 diabetes (she died, aged sixty-seven, of a heart attack linked to her condition), so I was minded to take my diagnosis seriously from the start. One of the difficulties of persuading people to act after diagnosis is the absence of symptoms early on.

Inspired by Michel Montignac's books and those of others, I adjusted my way of eating. Out went 'the whites' – white bread, white pasta and white rice – in other words, refined carbohydrates. Some root vegetables like potatoes, parsnips and beets are also best avoided, as they register high on the glycaemic index.

Rather than feeling deprived, this opened up new culinary paths – the discovery of the sweet potato, for instance. There are no excluded foods that I miss, though I don't have a sweet tooth, and I confess to looking for wholewheat pizzas on menus occasionally!

This adjustment, combined with regular walks and gentle yoga, reduced my blood-sugar levels significantly. For years I avoided taking medicine for diabetes, simply by improving my diet and increasing my level of exercise.

Type 2 diabetes is not curable, but it can be controlled without too much sacrifice.

Of course, it helped that I liked to cook. I had been a keen cook for years. That too goes back to my mother. I grew up in the 1940s and 1950s in post-war austerity Britain. Food rationing only came to an end in 1954, when I was twelve years old. (In America rationing ended eight years earlier in 1946!)

Robin Ellis (in the middle, in jacket and tie) with his parents, Tony and Molly, and siblings. Robin's mother had to inject herself daily as a result of Type 1 diabetes; she later died of a heart attack linked to the condition. Molly is holding Robin's youngest brother, Jack, who also grew up to become an actor. The middle brother, Peter, on the left, became a TV director.

My father worked for British Railways and had a modest income with a wife and three young boys to support, so Ma had to be a good manager of the food budget. I remember queuing with her at the Sainsbury's grocery store in Golders Green in north London for what seemed like hours. We would wait at one counter to buy half a pound of butter, then queue on the other side of the aisle for a pound of tomatoes and stand in yet another line for bacon. Is it too fanciful to suppose that waiting resentfully in all those lines unconsciously instilled in me an appreciation of quality and the importance of spending time searching it out?

Perhaps, but I do the same thing now, visiting our local French open-air markets at least three times a week, standing in queues at the cheese stall, the fishmonger, the organic vegetable grower. Buying local produce from the vendors I have come to know over a period of twenty years is one of the great pleasures of life in rural France. Our nearest town, Castres, has four open-air market days a week, plus another evening market for organic produce.

As well as being a good budget manager, my mother, Molly, was a good cook. She collected recipes from newspapers and magazines and pasted them into a large, blue foolscap notebook. She would also write out recipes and pass them on. I have her recipe for Smoked Mackerel Pâté (page 75), written in her clear flowing hand, pasted into my large *red* foolscap notebook. I collect recipes now and enjoy passing them on.

Molly loved to cook and to entertain. Thanks to her I grew up enjoying well-prepared simple food, eaten with family and friends around the kitchen table. She made her own marmalade with Seville oranges in February and started the traditional English Christmas pudding in September. We had individual Yorkshire puddings with roast beef on special Sundays with bread soaked in the 'goodness' – the natural juices from the joint.

Often on a Sunday night, I'd give her a break and cook my 'Special' – Macaroni Cheese with sliced tomato, grilled on top. I'd bring everything into the living room on a tray table. Brother Peter was just six in 1954 and would be in bed; brother Jack (also now an actor) wasn't on the scene until June the following year, so Ma, Dad and I would sit in front of the fire and listen to Mary Martin in *South Pacific* singing 'I'm Gonna Wash That Man Right Outa My Hair' on 78s on Dad's top-of-the-range gramophone.

Those convivial meals with my parents were the start of my love affair with food – and eating with others, in an agreeable social setting. In that same year, 1954, when rationing ended in Britain, Dad took advantage of concessionary rail travel for British Rail employees in Europe and took us all to the Costa Brava on Spain's Mediterranean coast for a two-week holiday. It was a bold destination for that era, long before British package tours hit the scene. I ate garlic for the first time, eggs cooked in olive oil, sun-ripened peaches and tomatoes unlike any we'd ever bought at Sainsbury's. This exposure to a completely different cuisine made a deep impression on me – and, of course, my mother.

We spent two weeks in Lloret de Mar, bizarrely sharing the beach and sun with Franco's military police, who wore strange helmets and carried menacing machine guns; very different from the beaches at Woolacombe Sands in Devon, or in Cornwall. As an impressionable twelve-year-old English schoolboy, I concluded that there was an interesting world elsewhere . . .

That year also saw the publication of Elizabeth David's seminal cookbook, *Italian Food* – a follow-up to her first book, *A Book of Mediterranean Food*. Her books were to underwrite a cooking revolution in Britain and have inspired me for years.

When you cook you're in control of what you eat. The fact that I liked to cook helped me negotiate the early days after the diagnosis with more confidence; it would be more problematic for someone not able or not keen to cook.

Cooking empowers – and is the key!

'The easiest and most pleasurable way to eat *well*, is to cook.'

Food writer Martha Rose Shulman in *The New York Times*

'No one is born a great cook, one learns by doing.'

Julia Child, American cook, food writer and legend

Cooking is not a mystery only to be understood by the trained and ordained few, though many of the cooking shows on TV might lead you to think that. There are exceptions, but so few of them are about encouraging us to get into the kitchen, break a few eggs and make omelettes. They are mainly aired and viewed as light entertainment. Cooking as a contest, professional or amateur – the turn-on is the competition, not the cooking. We can sit back and watch them do it and then send out for a takeaway!

It's true some people hate to cook. And there is not the same family cooking tradition in the Anglo-Saxon world as in the countries that border the Mediterranean, where even if the pressures of modern life threaten a break with the past and takeaways are taking over (McDonald's are popping up here like autumn mushrooms), 'Grandma's' cooking is firmly in the collective unconscious memory. Talking about food here in SW France is as compulsive as talking about the weather and considered as legitimate a subject for serious conversation at dinner as politics or religion – and usually safer!

Cooking is a daily ritual for me, sometimes a chore, but more often a pleasure. Shopping seasonally, lining up the ingredients, preparing them for the pot, grill or oven; then carrying out the recipe.

Step by step – an integral part of my everyday life.

Not everyone has the time, I know, but simple food is not hard to cook and nor are the recipes in this book – that's the point. Julia Child again:

'You don't have to cook fancy or complicated masterpieces – just good food from fresh ingredients.'

Robin Ellis, Lautrec, France

The key to the Mediterranean diet is always to use the best ingredients you can afford and find. Eating in is cheaper than eating out – so you can legitimately cut yourself some slack and spend a bit extra.

The Mediterranean Diet

RESEARCH NOW SHOWS THAT THE MEDITERRANEAN WAY OF EATING IS ONE OF THE HEALTHIEST ON THE PLANET. KEY ELEMENTS INCLUDE:

Eating plenty of fresh fruit and vegetables

Eating whole grains, brown rice, wholewheat pasta and legumes

Seasoning food with herbs and spices (so less salt is required)

Including nuts and seeds (dry roasting brings out the flavour)

Reducing the amount of red meat in the diet

Eating fish or shellfish at least twice a week

Limiting dairy products (use low-fat versions)

Cooking with olive oil rather than butter

Ever since eating those eggs in Spanish olive oil on the Costa Brava, I have always favoured olive oil over butter for cooking and, as you will see, I cook almost exclusively with it now. This always means cold processed Extra Virgin olive oil. Nowadays, I rarely like the flavour of butter in cooked food – though sometimes a mixture of oil and butter is useful.

Stock is a touchy subject in some households. It's simple for me: I have never got into the habit of making fresh stock. I've been using organic vegetable stock cubes (available in most health-food stores) for years and I use store-bought cubes and powder in these recipes. I no longer use chicken stock cubes; their flavour is too marked for me now, but it's a matter of taste; use the stock you like and trust. For those who have the time and energy to make homemade stock, I tip my hat in admiration.

It's important to taste food as it cooks, to judge the seasoning and the doneness. Sample the simmering tomato sauce to see if it's concentrated enough. Test the green bean to see how much longer it must cook. Bite on the strand of spaghetti to make sure it's done to your liking.

Be careful when handling fresh chillies as they can sting. Wash your hands thoroughly after handling them.

A pair of tongs is essential and a small wooden tasting spoon is a good idea too.

Eggs can be medium or large, whatever you have to hand.

American readers should follow the cup measurements (see conversion chart, page 220) when measuring volumes of liquid since UK (not US) pints are used in the recipes.

Bon appétit – Buon appetito!

With special thanks

to some of the professional cooks who have inspired me, starting with Elizabeth David, the wonderful Marcella Hazan, Mireille Johnston, Jenny Baker, Anna Del Conte, Valentina Harris, Rose Elliot, Claudia Roden and, more recently, Rose Gray and Ruth Rogers, Jamie Oliver and Nigel Slater.

Soups

Recently we've been enjoying soup for supper.
As the name suggests (*souper*: to have supper), this is the
traditional way of eating an evening meal. Eating lightly at the
end of the day is obviously better for the digestion and makes
it easier for the body to settle into the sleep mode.

Soups make a lovely lunch too – followed by a salad. Many
of the recipes here are quick and simple to make. They keep
well and the taste improves in the fridge, so they can be wheeled
out for company. Summer soups served chilled, such as
Donald's Cold Cucumber Soup (page 20), make life easier
when entertaining.

Donald Douglas, who, as Captain Malcolm McNeil, chased me in vain, through many *Poldark* episodes, has finally come to terms with the hopelessness of his pursuit and, in fact, lives close by. He's much better at making soup than he ever was as a soldier and, as a way of letting bygones be bygones, has given me permission to include this wonderful summer soup. You may wish you'd made more because this soup is something!

Donald's Cold Cucumber Soup

SERVES 5 (2 LADLES EACH)
2 tbsp olive oil
1 level tsp salt – be careful,
   the stock may be salty
2 garlic cloves, peeled and crushed
zest of a small lemon
juice of ½ lemon
1 large cucumber
500g/16oz yogurt
   (or 4 x 125g/4oz pots)
1 organic vegetable stock cube
2 tbsp chopped parsley,
   plus a little extra to garnish
5 ice cubes
10 peeled prawns (optional)

1 In a large bowl, mix together the olive oil, salt, garlic and lemon zest and juice.

2 Peel the cucumber, leaving some strips of green. Grate the cucumber into the bowl. Add the yogurt.

3 Make 350ml/12 fl oz stock with the stock cube.

4 When cool, add to the bowl. Add the chopped parsley and mix all the ingredients thoroughly.

5 Chill in the fridge, preferably overnight. It's a good idea to put the soup bowls in the fridge for a couple of hours before serving.

6 Stir the soup thoroughly and place an ice cube in each bowl. I like to add 2 peeled prawns and a pinch of parsley too.

This is adapted from Valentina Harris's *Recipes from an Italian Farmhouse*. It's wonderfully simple and the ingredients speak for its authenticity. Serve it over wholewheat or rye toast, stroked with a bruised clove of garlic.

Fennel Soup

SERVES 4

4 large bulbs of fennel, bruised bits
   removed, halved top to toe, then cut
   side down, each half finely sliced
3 garlic cloves, peeled and finely
   chopped
2 tbsp flat-leaved parsley, chopped
2 good tbsp olive oil
salt and pepper
1.2 litres/2 pints vegetable stock

1 Combine the fennel, garlic, parsley and olive oil in a large pan with a pinch of salt, and turn over in the oil.

2 Cook gently, turning to avoid burning, for about 7–8 minutes.

3 Add the stock and bring to the boil.

4 Simmer gently for 20 minutes or until the fennel is completely tender. Check for salt, and season generously with black pepper.

This is easy. Perfect after a winter walk; just looking at the colour warms you up. It's adapted from a recipe in *Leaves from our Tuscan Kitchen* by Janet Ross, which gives a peek into the day-to-day ways of cooking in a Tuscan villa in the late nineteenth century. You could dry-roast some pumpkin seeds to sprinkle on the top. Meredith suggests that sautéed bacon bits would be good too.

Pumpkin Soup

SERVES 2

1 medium onion, peeled and chopped
500g/1lb pumpkin, chopped with its
  skin on
2 tbsp olive oil
1 tsp coriander powder
½ tsp cumin powder
¼ tsp cayenne powder
salt and pepper
600ml/1 generous pint stock
chopped parsley, 2 slices rye bread and
  olive oil, to serve

1 Put the onion and the pumpkin pieces in a saucepan with the olive oil. Add the coriander, spices, 1 teaspoon salt and a few grinds of the peppermill. Turn everything over, cover and sweat over a low heat for 20 minutes to soften the vegetables.

2 Add the stock and cook uncovered for a further 20 minutes until the pumpkin is tender enough to liquidise.

3 Liquidise the mix. This is best done with a stick blender – it saves so much washing up!

4 A pinch of chopped parsley is a nice touch in each bowl. I cut up some rye bread, a slice each, into crouton-size pieces, sauté in a little olive oil and add a pinch each of salt and cumin powder.

This is *easy*.
Perfect after a
winter walk;
just looking
at the colour
warms you up.

Of course, minestrone is Italian for soup! Here's a version we often enjoy in the winter months, made with or without smoked bacon.

Minestrone Soup

SERVES 6

1 tbsp olive oil
100g/4oz smoked bacon, diced (optional)
1 large onion, peeled and chopped
2 large leeks, outer leaves removed, washed and sliced
2 celery stalks, bruised bits cut away, chopped
175g/6oz tinned or bottled white beans
275g/9oz tinned tomatoes
1 sweet potato, peeled and diced
1 large fennel bulb, outer layers removed, chopped in large dice
a few cabbage leaves (Savoy, if possible), torn up
900ml/1½ pints or more vegetable stock
a small handful of parsley, tied
salt and pepper
jug olive oil, to serve

1 Heat the olive oil in a large saucepan, big enough to fit all the ingredients, and add the bacon (if using). Let it brown gently.

2 Add the chopped onion, leeks and celery (start with these in the oil if not using the bacon), mix them in well and let them sweat for about 20 minutes. This slow sweating is what gives depth to the soup.

3 Add the beans to the sweated vegetables and mix them in. Do the same with the tomatoes, breaking them up a little.

4 Add the diced sweet potato and fennel.

5 Add the cabbage, stock and the tied parsley. Season and bring gently to simmer, then cover and cook at this gentle simmer for a good hour. The soup should be thick with vegetables. Add more stock if you need it.

6 Serve with a jug of the best olive oil you can muster.

This is simple to make and delicious – another comforting soup for winter.

Leek and Chickpea (Garbanzo Bean) Soup

SERVES 4
1kg/2lb leeks
3 tbsp olive oil
salt and freshly ground black pepper
500g/1lb (large jar or tin) chickpeas
   (garbanzo beans), drained and rinsed
900ml/1½ pints vegetable stock
75g/3oz Parmesan cheese, freshly
   grated, plus extra to serve

1 Prepare the leeks by cutting away the damaged brown tops, leaving as much of the green as possible and trimming the root ends. To wash them effectively, cut them down centrally from the top to just above the root and rinse thoroughly to clear any muddy residue. Slice them finely.

2 Heat the olive oil in a large saucepan and add the sliced leeks and a little salt – how much depends on the saltiness of the stock to come, so be careful. Cover the pan and sweat the leeks over a low heat for about 20 minutes until they are nicely softened.

3 Add the chickpeas and mix with the leeks.

4 Add the stock and cook uncovered for 15 minutes.

5 Take a couple of ladles from the pan, mash the mixture and return to the pan. Add the Parmesan and some freshly ground black pepper and mix in well.

6 Reheat and serve with more Parmesan on the side.

It's a fair bet my mother first tasted this traditional summer soup from Andalusia in 1954 when my parents took my brother and me to the Costa Brava for a fortnight's holiday. There were five hotels at that time in Lloret de Mar (500 plus now!). We stayed in one of them with a pretty courtyard, close to the beach.

Ma's Gazpacho

SERVES 4

1kg/2lb ripe tomatoes, chopped roughly, retaining their juice
½ large cucumber, peeled and diced
½ large red pepper, deseeded and diced
2 spring onions, chopped
3 garlic cloves, peeled and pulped in a mortar with 1 tsp salt
salt and pepper
3 tbsp red wine vinegar
2 tbsp olive oil
a few drops Tabasco (optional)
olive oil and fresh basil (if you have it), to serve

1 Put the chopped tomatoes, cucumber, pepper, spring onions and garlic in a food processor. Pulse them to a not-too-smooth finish. Empty this already-tasty mix into a bowl and adjust the seasoning with salt and pepper.

2 Stir in the red wine vinegar and olive oil. Add a few drops of Tabasco (a matter of taste). Chill for a couple of hours or overnight.

3 Serve – a ladle each is enough – with a whirl of olive oil and a pinch of chopped fresh basil (if using). I sometimes add an ice cube to each bowl.

This is my version of a serious bean soup from Marcella Hazan.

White Bean and Parsley Soup

SERVES 4

8 tbsp olive oil
1 garlic clove, peeled and chopped
2 tbsp parsley, chopped
1kg/2lb tinned or, preferably, bottled white beans, drained and rinsed
salt and pepper
250ml/9 fl oz vegetable stock
toasted wholewheat bread and a little olive oil, to serve

1 Sauté the garlic in the olive oil gently in a large saucepan until it colours.

2 Add the parsley and stir a couple of times. Mix in the beans, a teaspoon salt and a couple of grinds of the peppermill.

3 Cover and cook gently for about 5 minutes to warm through.

4 Remove a quarter of the beans and purée in a blender, then return with the stock to the pan. Simmer for another 5 minutes.

5 Check the seasoning. Serve the soup over the toast in each bowl, finishing with a swirl of olive oil.

Gazpacho

4 Large Tomatoes
1 onion
2 medium cucumbers
3 small Cloves Garlic
[...] oz jar pimentos.
[...] water
[...]spoons Lime Vinegar
[...] olive oil
Salt. Tabasco

Tomatoes, onion
Put into blender
garlic & vinegar
puréed adding some
[...] necessary. Add
[...] adjust
[...] cold

Summer soups
served chilled, make
life easier when
entertaining.

There is no potato, cream or cheese in this recipe adapted from one by Nigel Slater that I spotted in a newspaper; the key ingredient is smoked bacon. We had this for supper the other night and Meredith said, 'What is this? It's so creamy. It's not potatoes, is it? It's delicious.'

Smoky Cauliflower Soup

SERVES 4

1 tbsp olive oil
50g/2oz smoked bacon, chopped
2 garlic cloves, peeled and chopped
1 medium onion, peeled and chopped
1 large cauliflower
2 bay leaves
900ml/1½ pints stock
salt and pepper

1 Gently heat the olive oil in a frying pan and sauté the bacon until it colours a little. Add the garlic and onion. Cook the mix for 5 minutes until the onion has softened.

2 Meanwhile, break up the cauliflower into florets and add to a large saucepan. When ready, add the onion and bacon mix to the cauliflower along with the bay leaves and stock. Cover and bring to a simmer and cook for about 10 minutes until the cauliflower is tender.

3 Lift a third of the mix out of the pan with a slotted spoon and into a bowl, letting the liquid fall back into the pan. Liquidise the contents of the pan using a food processor or stick blender and test the seasoning. Add the set-aside florets and serve the soup hot.

This soup is adapted from The River Cafe's recipe. It is simple and satisfying, with a light green hue and creamy texture – a welcome addition to the summer courgette repertoire.

Courgette (Zucchini) Soup

SERVES 4

1kg/2lb courgettes (zucchini), as fresh as possible, washed and cut into 2.5-cm/1-in pieces
2 garlic cloves, peeled and chopped
2 tbsp olive oil
600ml/1 pint stock
salt and pepper
50g/2oz grated Parmesan cheese – add more to your taste
1 small pot (125g/4oz) yogurt
a handful each of chopped parsley and basil

1 Fry the courgettes and garlic in the olive oil for about 30 minutes, until they are very tender and browned a little.

2 Add the stock and bring to a gentle simmer for 5 minutes.

3 Season with salt and pepper – taking care with the salt, assuming there is salt in the stock. Let the soup cool a little.

4 Remove a quarter of the courgette pieces and liquidise the rest using a food processor or stick blender. Stir in the cheese and yogurt, followed by the parsley and basil.

5 Reheat gently. Check the seasoning and bring to a simmer.

6 Serve in warm bowls, with the reserved courgette pieces scattered on top.

This superb soup, based on a recipe by Marcella Hazan, is a meal in itself. It takes a little time but is well worth it.

Swiss Chard, White Bean and Pasta Soup

SERVES 4

500g/1lb Swiss chard, leaves separated from stalks

900ml/1½ pints water

1 tsp salt

6 tbsp olive oil

2 whole garlic cloves, peeled

2 anchovy fillets, mashed

1 sprig fresh rosemary

375g/12oz tinned or bottled white beans

black pepper

300ml/½ pint hot water with ½ stock cube dissolved in it

75g/3oz wholewheat pasta – penne, farfalle, fusilli, etc

30g/1oz grated Parmesan cheese

1 Soak and rinse the leaves and stalks of the chard – they must be clean. Cut the stalks into cork-length chunks and roughly chop the leaves.

2 Fill a large saucepan with water, add the salt and bring to the boil. Put in the chard stalks first and cook them for a couple of minutes. Add the leaves and cook, uncovered, for another 3 minutes, until tender.

3 Remove the chard from the pan, reserving all the liquid for later use. It will serve as a good part of the soup liquid. Roughly chop the chard.

4 Heat the olive oil in a large pan and add the garlic. When it has browned, take the pan off the heat and add the anchovies and rosemary. Stir for a couple of minutes to dissolve the anchovies. Remove the garlic and rosemary. Turn the heat back on low and add the chard leaves and stalks. Turn them in the oil and cook for a couple of minutes.

5 Add the beans, turn in the oil, and cook them for a couple of minutes.

6 Pepper well. Perhaps add salt but be careful as anchovies are salty.

7 Add the chard water and stock. When the water comes to the boil, add the pasta and cook, covered to prevent evaporation, until tender.

8 Turn off the heat, add the cheese and serve.

Light Lunches and Starters

Elizabeth David elegantly established her choice for the perfect light lunch with the title of her book, *An Omelette and a Glass of Wine*. Omelettes feature regularly at home in France at lunchtime, and a slice of freshly made courgette (zucchini) frittata makes a delicious starter. In summer, with the arrival of the green bean, the choice is expanded. A scattering of beans for each person (say, 100g/4oz) with some good olive oil drizzled over them while they are still warm, and a thin slice of interesting toast (wholewheat walnut, perhaps) would be enough, but you could add some halved cherry tomatoes, crumbled feta or mashed anchovies.

This is a lovely seasonal starter that can be prepared in advance and served with a couple of quartered cherry tomatoes and a drizzle of olive oil. Add a green salad for a light lunch.

Aubergine (Eggplant) Slices with Walnut and Garlic Spread

SERVES 4

2 large aubergines (eggplants)
salt
2 tbsp olive oil
2–3 tbsp red wine vinegar

SAUCE

3–4 garlic cloves, peeled and crushed with a little salt
2 tbsp olive oil
50g/2oz walnuts, shelled (if you do this yourself, take care that no pieces of shell get left with the nuts)
a handful of chopped parsley

1 Wash and cut the aubergines lengthways into 1-cm/½-in slices. Salt them lightly and place in a colander for an hour or so to drain off some of their bitter juice.

2 Dry them thoroughly and brush with olive oil on both sides. Preheat the oven to 240°C/475°F/Gas Mark 9.

3 Put the aubergines on well-oiled foil in a shallow oven tray. Cook on the top shelf of the oven for about 20 minutes to brown them, turning after 10 minutes.

4 While the aubergines are in the oven, make the sauce. Mix the crushed garlic with a tablespoon of olive oil. Chop the walnuts in a processor or pound them in a pestle and mortar.

5 Combine the garlic, olive oil and walnuts with the parsley in a bowl and add another tablespoon of oil. Mix well and check for salt.

6 Take the aubergines out of the oven, put them on a serving plate, brush with the wine vinegar and spread the delicious sauce on top. Serve cold.

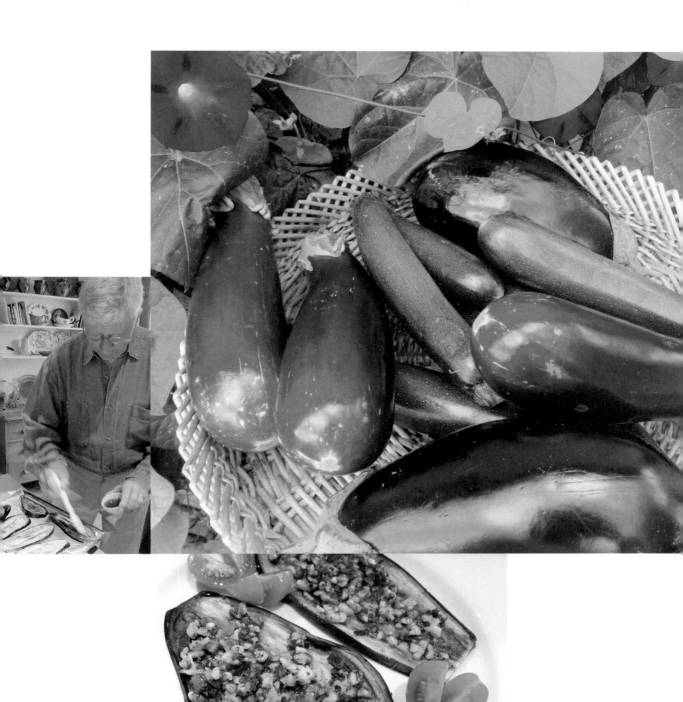

The combination of olive oil, rosemary, garlic and Parmesan is comforting and delicious. Served with a piece of wholewheat or rye toast, drizzled with olive oil, a poached egg and a simple salad, this makes an easy light lunch or supper.

Melting Tomatoes with Rosemary and a Parmesan Topping

SERVES 4

2 garlic cloves, peeled
2 stems of rosemary leaves, finely chopped
salt and pepper
2 tbsp olive oil, plus extra for brushing
10 medium ripe tomatoes, cut in half
3 tbsp grated Parmesan cheese, or more if needed

1 Preheat the oven to 200°C/400°F/Gas Mark 6. Put the garlic and rosemary together with a good pinch of salt and a few grindings of the peppermill in a mortar. Pulp with the pestle, then add the olive oil and stir to make a rough paste.

2 Cover a shallow oven tray with foil and brush it with oil. Place the tomatoes on it, cut-side up. Using a teaspoon, smooth a little of the garlicky paste on each tomato half.

3 Place the tray on the top rack of the oven and cook for about 20–30 minutes – the tomatoes should have softened and collapsed somewhat.

4 Remove from the oven and place a small pile of Parmesan on top of each tomato half. Put the tray back in the oven for about 15 minutes, until the cheese has browned on top.

Our friend Fronza Woods, who is vegetarian and cooks delicious delicacies, introduced us to these little numbers. They serve as a vegetable side dish or as a starter with a tomato coulis.

Courgette (Zucchini) Muffins

SERVES 6 AS A STARTER

2 courgettes (zucchini), unpeeled and grated
2 tbsp Emmental cheese, grated
4 tbsp grated onion
1 tbsp fine breadcrumbs, wholewheat or rye
salt and pepper
2 eggs
olive oil for brushing
tomato coulis (page 70), to serve

1 Preheat the oven to 200°C/400°F/Gas Mark 6.

2 Combine the courgettes, Emmental, onion and breadcrumbs, season well and mix thoroughly.

3 Check the seasoning and fold in the eggs.

4 Oil 6 muffin cups. This amount is enough to fill one of those rubber trays of 12. Fill each cup with the mixture and carefully place in the middle of the oven. Bake for 30–40 minutes. They should be springy and nicely brown. Serve on top of a tablespoon of tomato coulis.

Three medium courgettes (zucchini) from the single plant in the garden and five eggs made up this handy end-of-season dish adapted from Antonio Carluccio's *Vegetables* book. More scrambled eggs than omelette or frittata, it's a handy way to deal with the pile of courgettes waiting their turn as the glut develops – another is the courgette soup on page 29.

Courgette (Zucchini) Eggs

SERVES 4 AS A LIGHT LUNCH
3 medium courgettes (zucchini)
salt and pepper
3 tbsp olive oil, plus extra to serve
1 onion, peeled and thinly sliced
4 eggs
50g/2oz Parmesan cheese, grated
2 tbsp parsley, chopped
1 tbsp mint (if available), chopped
8 pieces wholewheat bread, to serve

1 To prepare the courgettes, peel them in stripes, quarter them lengthways and cut them into dice. Sprinkle with salt and leave to drain in a sieve or colander for an hour or so. Dry on kitchen paper or a tea towel.

2 Heat the olive oil in a pan big enough to hold all the courgettes in a single layer. Sauté the onion over a low heat until it softens and then add the courgettes, turning them over in the oil. Cook until they are tender – about 20 minutes.

3 Meanwhile, break the eggs into a mixing bowl and whisk them together. Mix in the Parmesan, parsley and mint (if using) and season with salt and pepper – more pepper than salt, bearing in mind the courgettes have already been salted.

4 Pour the egg mix over the courgettes and start turning it over gently over a low heat as the eggs solidify. This will not take long. It's ready when the mix is loosely solid – scrambled, in fact! Take care not to let it become *too* solid!

5 To serve, Meredith toasts 2 pieces of wholewheat bread per person to act as elegant shovels(!) and drizzles some olive oil over them.

To serve, Meredith toasts 2 pieces of wholewheat bread per person to act as elegant shovels . . .

Asparagus is wonderful, but even in its short season it can get a bit repetitive! This is a handy alternative way to serve; it's quick and easy too. The addition of thyme comes from *The River Cafe Pocket Book: Salads & Vegetables*.

Roast Asparagus

SERVES 4
2 tbsp olive oil, plus extra to serve
500g/1lb asparagus
2 tbsp fresh thyme leaves
salt

1 Preheat the oven to 220°C/425°F/Gas Mark 7.

2 Heat the olive oil in a shallow baking tray.

3 Turn the asparagus in it, sprinkle over the thyme and some salt. The roasting time depends on the thickness of the asparagus: about 5 or 6 minutes for thin and a bit longer for the thicker stems. It should crisp up a bit.

4 Serve with extra oil and salt, or you could try it with the simple sauce for fish on page 73.

A traditional North African favourite, this version is adapted from a recent discovery in Yotam Ottolenghi's sumptuous vegetable cookbook *Plenty*. The name means 'mixture' in Tunisian Arabic; I think it's better to stick to Shakshuka! It is often served in individual cast iron pans, which I imagine adds to the pleasure: *one pan, and all for me!*

Shakshuka (Red Pepper Stew with Eggs)

SERVES 2

½ tsp cumin seeds
60ml/2 fl oz olive oil
1 large red or yellow onion, peeled and sliced
2 red peppers, washed, deseeded and thinly sliced
1 bay leaf
thyme leaves from a few sprigs
2 tbsp parsley
3 large fresh ripe or tinned tomatoes, roughly chopped with the juices
60ml/2 fl oz water
¼ tsp cayenne pepper
pinch (few strands) saffron
salt and pepper
2 or 4 eggs (your choice)
2 pieces wholewheat toast, to serve

1 Dry-roast the cumin seeds for a minute or two in a medium pan, taking care not to burn them.

2 Add the olive oil to the pan and heat. Cook the onion over a medium heat for 5 minutes to soften it.

3 Add the peppers and herbs and turn everything over thoroughly. Cover the pan for 5 minutes to start the softening of the peppers. Cook for a further 5 minutes uncovered.

4 Add the tomatoes and the water, a little at a time to avoid diluting the sauce, the cayenne and saffron and season with salt and pepper. Cook for 15 minutes on a low heat, covering for a short time if you think the peppers need further softening. The result should be a lightly spiced sauce in which to poach the eggs.

5 Carefully break the eggs (2 or 4, your choice) into the sauce, leaving space between them. Cover the pan and cook over a lowish heat until the eggs are cooked to your liking. Serve with pieces of wholewheat toast.

A *frittata* is an Italian omelette, made the opposite way to a French omelette; the 'trick' is in the time it takes. It's cooked over the lowest heat, for about 20 minutes; a French omelette is cooked over the highest heat, for less than a minute! The French version is fluffy, the Italian firm but not dry, more like a pastry-less quiche served in slices. What they have in common is that you can fill them with pretty much whatever you fancy. Here, I've chosen a mix of cooked spinach and sautéed red onion. Other options are courgettes (zucchini) and onions, green beans, tomatoes, artichokes, plain cheese, or onions alone.

Spinach and Red Onion Frittata

SERVES 4 AS LUNCH, 6 AS A STARTER
300g/10oz spinach, washed and
　shaken free of water
salt and pepper
3 tbsp olive oil
1 medium red onion, peeled and sliced
6 eggs
50g/2oz Parmesan cheese, grated
½ tsp grated nutmeg
green salad, to serve

1 Put the spinach in a large saucepan over a low heat. There will be enough water clinging to the leaves to cook it down. Salt lightly as you put it in the pan. Let it reduce down. Transfer to a colander to drain and cool.

2 In a small frying pan, heat a tablespoon of the olive oil and sauté the onion gently until it starts to caramelise.

3 Squeeze the spinach free of water, without squeezing the life out of it! Loosen it up, separating it a little, then turn it over in the pan with the onion and season lightly with salt and pepper. Set aside to cool.

4 Break the eggs into a mixing bowl and whisk them. Fold in the spinach and onion mix and turn it all together thoroughly. Mix in the cheese and nutmeg. Season again lightly with salt and pepper.

5 Heat the remaining oil in a 25cm/10in pan. When it's hot add the egg mixture, spreading it evenly over the base. Turn the heat down to the lowest setting and let it cook for about 20 minutes on this very low heat. Use a heat diffuser if you think it's not low enough.

6 Fifteen minutes into cooking turn on the grill. Test the top of the frittata. When there's only a small pool of the mix left on top, it is ready to go under the grill – briefly – to finish. It shouldn't take much more than a minute under the grill to come out a little browned on top. Serve with a green salad.

Squeeze the spinach free of water, *without squeezing the life out of it!*

Based on Marcella Hazan's version of a classic, this is a very useful recipe as it doesn't use pastry. You can cook the spinach, rice and onion well in advance – the night before even – which means it turns into an assembly job and as such is therapeutic!

Rice and Spinach Torte

SERVES 4 AS LUNCH, MORE AS
A STARTER

1kg/2lb spinach, washed carefully
200g/7oz basmati long-grain rice
1 medium onion, peeled and chopped
30g/1oz butter
4 tbsp olive oil, plus extra as needed
¼ tsp grated nutmeg
50g/2oz grated Parmesan cheese
salt and pepper
5 eggs
30g/1oz breadcrumbs – rye or
    100 per cent wholewheat

1 Cook the spinach in the water clinging to it after washing, covered, over a gentle heat until it has wilted completely – about 10 minutes.

2 When it's cool enough, squeeze as much water out of the spinach as you can and roughly chop it.

3 Cook the rice as per the recipe on page 218. Drain and leave to cool.

4 Fry the onion in the butter and oil in a large sauté pan over a medium heat until it is a lively brown.

5 Add the cooled spinach and rice to the onion and cook over low heat for about 4 minutes, turning to mix and coat well with the oil and butter. Leave to cool.

6 Preheat the oven to 230°C/450°F/Gas Mark 8.

7 Add the nutmeg and half the cheese to the mixture. Season this mix carefully with salt and pepper – tasting and turning as you go – the salt should just come through. Break in the eggs one at a time, turning with each addition.

8 Oil a loose-bottomed 25cm/10in torte (oven) tin and sprinkle half the breadcrumbs over the base. Now turn the mix into it and smooth over the surface. Mix together the remaining crumbs and cheese and sprinkle them over the mix. Drizzle olive oil over the top.

9 Bake in the top of the oven for 15 minutes.

10 Serve tepid, perhaps with a tomato sauce.

Haricot verts (green beans) are perennial favourites here. Alice, our generous French neighbour, delivered a bagful, freshly picked this morning from her pottage. We'll eat them today unadorned, apart from a little salt and a swirl of the best olive oil we have. This recipe is a handy alternative. Our friend, Jane, who made it for us recently, reminded me that the recipe is based on one in the little vegetable book from the River Cafe collection. The beans are lightly coated with an anchovy and caper sauce with sweet cherry tomato quarters and basil added. If you are not keen on anchovies, leave them out.

Green Beans with Tomatoes and Anchovies

SERVES 4

500g/1lb green beans, connecting tops nipped off

salt and pepper

4 tbsp finest olive oil, plus extra if needed

juice of 1 lemon

8 anchovy fillets, snipped into bits with a pair of scissors

1 tbsp capers – fat ones are best

a handful of Niçoise olives, pitted

a handful of ripe cherry tomatoes, carefully quartered – watch your fingers!

1 Cook the beans in plenty of salted water until just tender – hoist one out to test.

2 Drain, put in a mixing bowl and coat with 2 tablespoons of olive oil (the best you have available).

3 In another bowl, combine the lemon juice and the remaining 2 tablespoons of olive oil.

4 Snip the anchovy fillets into the bowl and add the capers and the pitted olives. Season with salt and black pepper, bearing in mind the saltiness of the anchovies and olives. Add another tablespoon of olive oil, if needed.

5 Spoon this sauce over the beans and mix.

6 Carefully transfer the beans to a favourite serving plate and scatter over the tomatoes.

Salads

Salad can mean pretty much anything these
days – imagination is the mother of invention! The other day,
on the recommendation of a friend, I ordered the mushroom
salad from an Italian menu. It was a simple idea, involving small
field mushrooms, finely sliced shavings of Parmesan, some fresh
thyme and a dressing of olive oil and lemon juice, with rocket
(arugula) leaves worked in, seasoned with salt and pepper. That
was lunch and very good it was. There are classic salads too, of
course, and many ways of assembling them. In this section I've
included some particularly useful ones: Tonno e Fagioli and
Salade Niçoise are a meal in themselves, for instance, and in
summer it's likely you will have the ingredients for a Greek Salad
in the fridge. See pages 213–214 in the Sundries section for salad
dressing ideas.

One of my all-time favourite salads, this is a good standby. There's usually a tin of tuna and bottle of white beans in the larder, then all you need is a small red onion, oil and vinegar. No cooking is involved and it's all ready in 15 minutes.

Tonno e Fagioli (Tuna and White Bean Salad)

SERVES 4–6

2 x 160g/5½oz tins good tuna in olive oil – there should be enough, i.e. don't stint

2 x 400g/13oz tins or bottles (I prefer bottles) white beans (haricots blancs, cannellini)

3 tsp red wine vinegar

6 tbsp olive oil

salt and pepper

½ red onion, peeled and very thinly sliced

chopped parsley, if you have it

green salad (optional), to serve

1 Drain the tuna. Drain and rinse the beans.

2 Whisk the vinegar, olive oil and salt and pepper into a vinaigrette.

3 Put the beans, tuna and onion into a bowl and pour over the sauce. Mix all the ingredients thoroughly, turning them over carefully. Taste and add more seasoning and more oil if necessary.

4 Sprinkle over the parsley (if using). This dish works well on its own, however a green salad makes for a nice colour contrast on the plate.

One of my all-time
favourite salads . . .

This can also serve as a delicious relish for salmon.

Cucumber and Red Onion Salad

SERVES 4 AS A SIDE SALAD
1 large cucumber, peeled and thinly
  sliced (a food processor disc
  saves time)
1 small red onion, peeled and
  thinly sliced
salt and pepper

DRESSING
1 tbsp cider vinegar
1 tsp Dijon mustard
1 tbsp chopped parsley or dill

1 Combine the prepared cucumber and red onion and sprinkle with salt. Let the mix drain in a colander or sieve for 30 minutes or longer.

2 Spread the mix over a layer of kitchen paper, cover with a second layer and press down gently to lift off excess liquid. Transfer it to a favourite plate or bowl.

3 Whisk the vinegar and mustard together with some pepper and fold in the chopped parsley or dill. Pour this over the cucumber and onion and turn it all over.

4 Leave it to luxuriate in the mix for an hour in the fridge.

I'm serving this today with the salmon fishcakes (page 119) – it should cut through their richness nicely.

Fennel Salad with Parmesan Shavings

SERVES 4

4 fennel bulbs, tough outer
  layers removed
4 tbsp olive oil
1 lemon, juice and zest
Parmesan cheese shavings
salt and pepper
a handful of chopped parsley

1 Halve the fennel bulbs and lay the cut side down flat. Slice these halves finely and put in a bowl.

2 Whisk the olive oil and lemon juice together and pour over the fennel bulbs.

3 Add some Parmesan shavings, enough for flavour but not to overwhelm.

4 Season generously but with care, tasting as you go.

5 Turn the salad over several times to coat everything in the mix.

6 Turn into a serving bowl.

7 Sprinkle the chopped parsley, some extra shavings of Parmesan and the lemon zest on top and set aside to marinate for perhaps an hour, if there's time.

Greek Salad

Tomatoes, cucumber (peeled or unpeeled), sweet (red) onion, green or red peppers (optional), black olives, feta cheese, olive oil, red wine vinegar, salt and pepper. A blue sky, a dry summer heat, a swimming pool or blue, blue sea and a glass of retsina . . . The first nine ingredients are essential (ten if you include the peppers), the last five preferable but not obligatory!

Red, pink, pale green, black and white are the colours looking up at you from the bowl on the table. It works best if the tomatoes and cucumber are sun-ripe and juicy, but the contrasting tastes of the feta, olives, olive oil, vinegar and seasoning make this national dish worth eating any time, anywhere.

In Greece, chunks, curls, slices and slabs lend a spirit of generosity to the brimming bowls presented. Chunks of tomato, curls of soft red onion, slices – thickish – of cucumber and peppers (optional) and slabs of feta, the last laid on top of the finished construction like small white tombstones.

The olives in Greece are the Kalamata variety, similar to the small black olives that feature in that other summer wonder – *salade Niçoise*. Their faint bitterness balances the sweetness of the tomatoes and cucumber. The juicy black *olives Grecque*s from our market are a meaty alternative.

Add the dressing, turn the contents over and your fork will start jabbing in – involuntarily.

'Kali Orexi!'
'Buon appetito!'
'Bon appétit!'

Rocket (arugula) is available everywhere these days. If you have the space, it's quick to grow – forty days from seed to plate. We eat a lot of it! It makes an attractive base for this simple salad from Lombardy, spotted in Paola Gavin's *Italian Vegetarian Cookery*.

Simple Rocket (Arugula), Tomato and Goats' Cheese Salad

SERVES 2–3

a couple of handfuls of rocket
   (arugula) leaves
½ red onion, peeled and sliced as thinly
   as you can manage
2 largish tomatoes, not too
   thickly sliced
a few juicy black olives, pitted
a small goats' cheese, broken into
   smallish pieces

DRESSING

1 tbsp red wine vinegar
3 tbsp olive oil
salt and pepper

1 Spread the rocket over the base of your favourite salad bowl. Add the onion.

2 Follow with the tomatoes, olives and cheese.

3 Whisk the dressing ingredients together and pour the vinaigrette over the salad. Toss just before serving.

A lovely traditional salad from southwest France. The Roquefort caves, where the famous sheeps' cheeses are aged, are not far from us. One day we'll visit. Walnuts are seriously healthy eating! Here, they are toasted and make a wonderful foil to the richness of the cheese.

Green Salad with Roquefort Cheese and Dry-roasted Walnuts

SERVES 4 AS A STARTER

50g/2oz walnuts
1 large frisée lettuce
½ sweet onion, peeled and sliced
100g/4oz Roquefort cheese, roughly broken up

DRESSING

salt and pepper
1 tbsp red wine vinegar
3 tbsp olive oil
1 tsp walnut oil, if you have it

1 Crack open the walnuts and separate the nuts from the shells, taking care not to include any tooth-threatening pieces of shell. Dry-roast the kernels over a gentle flame in a small frying pan until they colour and give off the lovely aroma associated with dry-roasted nuts.

2 Wash and spin-dry the salad leaves and add them to a large mixing bowl. Add the nuts and the onion slices.

3 To make the dressing, put a pinch of salt in a small mixing bowl and mix in the vinegar. Add the two oils and whisk it all together.
Add the cheese to the salad and spoon vinaigrette over the top. Turn it all over carefully and thoroughly.

4 Portion the salad out onto small plates beforehand or pass the bowl round the table, allowing people to serve themselves.

The flattened, strong, textured whorls of varying shades of green of a whole Escarole lettuce invite strong treatment, which it gets in this adaptation of a wonderful *Moro Cookbook* recipe.

Salad of Escarole Lettuce with Spicy Chorizo

SERVES 4

leaves from an Escarole lettuce,
    washed and spun dry
1 tbsp olive oil
200g/7oz spicy chorizo sausage,
    cut in half lengthways and diced
120ml/4 fl oz dry sherry
2 tbsp parsley, chopped

DRESSING

½ tsp Dijon mustard
1 tbsp red wine vinegar
1 small garlic clove, peeled and crushed
4 tbsp olive oil

1 Put the Escarole leaves in a salad bowl.

2 Heat the olive oil in a small frying pan and cook the sausage over a medium heat until it begins to brown nicely.

3 Pour in the sherry and continue cooking until it burns off.

4 Scatter over the parsley.

5 Mix the dressing ingredients together and pour over the salad, then add the sausage pieces. Turn it all over carefully and serve.

A wonderfully useful salad for company on sunny days in summer, everyone has their version of this classic. For me, the essentials are anchovies, eggs, olives, beans, tuna and ripe tomatoes, plus a fair amount of garlic in the dressing.

Salade Niçoise

SERVES 4

crisp salad leaves, enough to cover base
   of serving bowl
4 ripe tomatoes, peeled if you prefer
(pour boiling water over them and
   leave for 30 seconds) and quartered
½ large cucumber, peeled, quartered
   lengthwise and deseeded
1 large or several small spring onions,
   finely sliced
250g/8oz green beans, cooked to
   just tender
2–3 tins tuna, drained weight about
   200–300g/7–10oz
a handful of Niçoise or other
   black olives
8 anchovy fillets
4 freshly hard-boiled eggs, halved

DRESSING

8 tbsp olive oil
2 garlic cloves, peeled and mashed
salt and pepper
some basil, parsley and mint leaves –
   whatever's available

1 Choose a serving dish large enough for a pretty display. Make a base of the salad leaves, followed by the tomatoes, cucumber and onion, and build from there. The eggs should be added last, with a slice of anchovy on each half.

2 Whisk the olive oil and garlic together, add the salt and pepper and the herbs, and pour over the salad.

3 Show off your handiwork. Then carefully turn over the salad in the dressing and serve – with a chilled rosé perhaps.

A sparklingly fresh salad to complement and at the same time cut through the rich oiliness of the Baked Mackerel Fillets (page 112) we are having for lunch today.

Fennel, Radish, Spring Onion and Celery Salad

SERVES 2–3

1 large fennel bulb
1 large spring onion
1 long celery stick, finely sliced
several large red radishes, finely sliced
1–2 tbsp lightly pan-roasted sunflower seeds (optional)
chopped parsley, to garnish

DRESSING

juice of 1 lemon
3–4 tbsp good olive oil
salt and pepper

1 Remove the outer leaves of the fennel bulb, cut in half on the vertical and slice finely.

2 Remove the outer layer of the spring onion, cut in half on the vertical and slice finely.

3 Combine the raw vegetables in a bowl and add some sunflower seeds, if you have them.

4 To make the dressing, whisk together the juice of the lemon with the best olive oil you have and season with salt and pepper.

5 Add the dressing to the vegetable salad, turning turn everything over carefully so the dressing gets to visit all corners! Serve with a generous sprinkling of chopped parsley.

Adapted from an early Nigel Slater recipe, this is very handy as a quick standby when you feel at a loss for something to serve for a light lunch.

Tuna Salad

SERVES 4

2 x 200g/7oz tins tuna, drained and flaked
1 tbsp Dijon mustard
3 tbsp tarragon vinegar
6 tbsp olive oil
125g pot yogurt, drained a little using a sieve parked on a bowl, then whisked smooth
2 tbsp parsley, finely chopped, plus extra to garnish
2 tbsp chives, finely chopped
2 tbsp chervil, finely chopped (a plus if you can find it)
salt and pepper
½ cucumber, peeled, quartered, deseeded and finely diced
2 spring onions, finely chopped
1 tbsp sunflower seeds, lightly toasted
crisp green lettuce, to serve

1 Put the tuna into a favourite serving bowl.

2 Whisk together the mustard, vinegar, olive oil, yogurt, parsley, chives, chervil and a pinch each of salt and pepper into a thick sauce.

3 Add the cucumber, spring onions and sunflower seeds.

4 Pour the sauce over the tuna and carefully turn over all the ingredients.

5 Sprinkle over the remaining parsley and serve with crisp green lettuce leaves.

Sauces and Dips

Some sauces are for dipping too, and some dips can serve as sauces. So I've combined them! Apart from the Quick Tomato Sauce (page 70), none of the sauces requires cooking; each is assembled from high-quality fresh ingredients and designed to complement, not overwhelm or mask. The same goes for the dips – only Baba Ganoush (page 74) needs cooking. 'Dips' often turn into scoops or even shovelfuls: if they are tasty, they are moreish and if you aren't careful, there's no room left for lunch!

Two neighbours came for supper the other night and I tried out a spicy chicken dish. It didn't impress Meredith, and our friends were polite but didn't exactly rave. I served this yogurt sauce with it, which I think *is* very tasty, as well as useful. I noticed Meredith tucking into it the next day with a fennel salad!

Cumin Yogurt Sauce

SERVES 4
3 x 125g/4oz pots organic yogurt
1 garlic clove, peeled
½ tsp salt
1 tsp cumin powder
1 tbsp olive oil

1 Whisk the yogurt until smooth to make it a bit thicker, then drain through a sieve into a bowl (see page 216) for half an hour or so.

2 Pulp the garlic in a pestle and mortar with the salt. Add the cumin and mix it in thoroughly. Fold in the olive oil.

3 Add this mix to the yogurt and whisk well to combine. Refrigerate until you are ready to serve.

This is adapted from Rena Salaman's lovely and authentic *Greek Food*. It's a refreshing garlicky sauce that goes particularly well with grilled summer vegetables, chicken and lamb.

Tzatziki

SERVES 4– 5
480ml/16 fl oz organic yogurt, wrapped in muslin and squeezed gently to drain it a little, or left overnight in a sieve to drain into a bowl (see page 216)
2 tbsp olive oil
2 tsp white wine or cider vinegar
2 garlic cloves, peeled and pulped in a mortar with a little salt
2 fresh mint leaves, finely chopped
¼ medium cucumber, peeled, quartered lengthways, deseeded and finely chopped
salt and pepper

1 Carefully scrape the drained yogurt into a mixing bowl and whisk smooth.

2 In a separate small bowl, whisk the olive oil and vinegar together. Mix in the garlic and the mint.

3 Fold this into the yogurt, then add the cucumber. Season lightly, taste and adjust the seasoning, then refrigerate until needed.

This to my mind is so much nicer than traditional mint sauce. The apple and onion put a real spring into its step – helped on by the cider vinegar. Goes wonderfully with roast lamb or lamb chops.

Mint Sauce with Apple and Onion

SERVES 4
a good handful of leaves from a
   large bunch of mint
1 apple, peeled, cored and
   roughly chopped
1 small onion, peeled and quartered
salt
a good splash of cider vinegar

1 Process the mint, apple and onion in a blender – not too finely, it should have texture.

2 Add some salt and a good splash of vinegar. Taste to see if it needs a little more of anything – it may take a couple of tries to get the balance right. Then leave to marinate in the fridge until it's needed.

3 Remove from the fridge and bring back to room temperature before serving.

This is a new one on me. I like the name – which can be loosely translated as 'made up of various ingredients put together in no particular order'! (There is a song from *Mary Poppins* that includes the words 'chim-chim cher-ee' – I doubt there's a connection, though!) It makes a change from the mint sauce traditionally served with lamb and is good with grilled chicken and fish too. The first time I made it I didn't have fresh coriander (cilantro) so I used double the amount of parsley.

Chimichurri – Argentine Parsley Sauce

SERVES 2
1 garlic clove, peeled
1 tsp salt
4 tbsp chopped parsley
4 tbsp chopped fresh coriander
   (cilantro)
a few grinds of pepper
2 tbsp chopped red onion
1 tbsp capers, rinsed
1 tbsp white wine, red wine or
   cider vinegar
3 tbsp olive oil
grilled lamb chops or roast chicken,
   to serve

1 Pulp the garlic and salt in a pestle and mortar.

2 Put all the ingredients, except the olive oil, in a food processor and pulse while slowly adding the oil to make a loose but not sloppy sauce.

3 Transfer to a pretty jug or bowl and serve with grilled lamb chops or roast chicken.

Adapted from the first *River Cafe Cook Book*, this is very useful for spreading on grilled aubergines (eggplant) or to accompany tuna, mackerel or salmon.

Quick Tomato Sauce

MAKES 800G/28OZ
3 garlic cloves, peeled and
    finely sliced
4 tbsp olive oil
2 x 800g/28oz tins tomatoes,
    drained of their juice
salt and pepper
a handful of fresh basil if you
    have some, chopped

1 Fry the garlic gently in 2 tablespoons of olive oil in a large pan but do not let it brown.

2 Add the tomatoes (break them up with a wooden spoon), a teaspoon of salt and a few grinds of the peppermill. Cook over a high heat, stirring frequently to prevent the sauce burning and watch out for splattering. Use the biggest wooden spoon you have.

3 When little red pockmarks appear, making it look as though the surface of the moon has turned red, you know it is almost there. The mixture will have reduced considerably to form a thick sauce with very little liquid left. This will take about 20 minutes. Add the last two tablespoons of olive oil and the basil, taste and check the seasoning.

4 To turn this into a coulis (puréed sauce), let it cool slightly, then work it through a sieve – this takes a little time. Then reheat it. A tablespoonful on a plate looks like a deep red setting sun

This version has a bit of a kick to it. There's garlic, cumin and cayenne in the mix – with olive oil and lemon juice to loosen it.

Hummus

SERVES 4–6
250g/8oz cooked chickpeas (garbanzo
    beans) (I prefer those in jars), drained
    and rinsed
3 garlic cloves, peeled and chopped,
    then pulped with ½ tsp salt
½ tsp salt
3 tbsp tahini paste (usually available
    in jars at good grocery stores or
    healthfood shops)
1 tsp cumin powder
½ tsp cayenne pepper
2 tbsp olive oil
juice of 2 lemons

1 Put all the ingredients except the lemon juice in a food processor and whizz until smooth.

2 Add half the lemon juice and taste.

3 Add more lemon juice to your taste.

This is a stunner and goes well with salmon fillet or chicken. You need a decent pile of herbs. Use whatever is available, with parsley, mint and chives as the base.

Green Sauce

1 bunch parsley
1 bunch mint
2 bunches chives
1 bunch chervil or tarragon
1 tbsp capers
salt and pepper
2 garlic cloves, peeled and sliced
   wafer-thin
1 tbsp Dijon mustard
2 lemons, juiced
200ml/7 fl oz olive oil

1 Pile the herbs together and chop them roughly.

2 Add the capers, salt and garlic to the pile and chop thoroughly.

3 Put this in a bowl and mix in the mustard, lemon juice and the olive oil. Season with pepper.

4 Taste it for the balance of lemon and olive oil; you should end up with a rough mush, a delicious-looking green mess!

Tarata! Taraahh! I've heard this described as a yogurt soup from Bulgaria and a sauce from Lebanon. My version is loose, lemony and lightly garlicky, to be enjoyed as a sauce spooned over or served on the side with meat or vegetables.

Tarator

SERVES 2
3 tbsp tahini
2 tbsp lemon juice
1 garlic clove, peeled and pulped in
   a mortar with ½ tsp salt
⅓ tsp cumin powder
4 tbsp water, plus extra if needed
1 tbsp parsley, chopped
salt

1 Put the tahini, lemon juice, garlic, cumin and water in a food processor and whizz to a smooth, runny consistency, adding a little more water if the sauce is too thick.

2 Stir in the chopped parsley and add salt to your taste.

A recipe for serving with white fish such as sea bass or hake – grilled or roasted. You could try adding some finely chopped mint leaves and a little very finely sliced garlic.

Simple Sauce

SERVES 4
4 tbsp olive oil
juice of 1 lemon
salt and pepper

1 Whisk all the ingredients together and empty into a small serving jug.

Based on Mireille Johnston's recipe – she got the mix just right – this is a traditional spread. The word originates from the Provençal for 'caper'. It's a great standby to have in the fridge and as far as making it goes, it is simplicity itself. You can serve it as a summer lunch on toast brushed with olive oil with a slice of the ripest tomato on top, on grilled slices of courgettes (zucchini) or aubergines (eggplant), or on savoury biscuits or small pieces of toast as an appetiser – or whatever! It is a favourite at St Martin – and would even persuade Cal McRae to come to lunch!

Tapenade

SERVES 4
200g/7oz black olives, the oily fleshy
   Greek ones are best, carefully pitted
   (it's important to use the plumpest,
   tastiest olives)
6 anchovy fillets, chopped
2 tbsp capers
2 garlic cloves, peeled and crushed
1 tsp fresh thyme
1 tbsp Dijon mustard
juice of 1 lemon
black pepper
120ml/4 fl oz olive oil

1 Put all the ingredients except the olive oil in a food processor. Using the surge button, gradually pour in the oil, bringing it to a nice nobbly sludge – i.e. not too smooth.

2 Taste for balance; you may need a little more lemon juice.

3 Pour into a bowl or plastic box, and drizzle a little more olive oil over the top to form a preserving film. Store in the fridge.

I have fallen in love with Baba Ganoush! First, there's the name – like a favourite childhood comforter. Then there's the smoky taste and creamy texture. Aubergines (eggplant) are singed on a burner here for a smoky flavour (sometimes roasted in the oven as well), then peeled when completely soft. You can leave out the burner bit and roast them in the oven; it just won't taste as smoky.

Baba Ganoush

SERVES 4

2 large aubergines (eggplants)
3 tbsp tahini paste (usually available in jars at good grocery stores or healthfood shops)
2 garlic cloves, peeled and pulped in a mortar with a pinch of salt
juice of 1 lemon
2 tbsp olive oil (optional)
1 tsp salt
toasted bread and green salad, to serve

1 Make a couple of slits in the aubergines – to avoid explosions! Balance the aubergines, one after the other, on top of a low gas flame or under a medium grill, turning regularly to singe and soften them. The time it takes will depend on the size of the aubergine. The flesh should be very soft.

2 Preheat the oven to 200°C/400°F/Gas Mark 6 if you choose to roast the aubergines. Put the aubergines on a shallow oven tray and on the top shelf of the oven for 40 minutes, or until they have collapsed and the flesh is soft inside.

3 Let them cool down. Peel them carefully and transfer the flesh to a large bowl.

4 Mix in the tahini, garlic, lemon juice, olive oil (if using) and salt, making a smoothish mash. Taste and add more salt, lemon juice and olive oil as needed. Spread thickly on toast and serve with a green salad for the perfect light lunch.

My mother Molly cooked for us every day on a small budget in the late 1940s and '50s. She was resourceful and adventurous – not afraid to try new recipes inspired by trips abroad. From her I learnt that it was worth spending a little time in the kitchen – not least because I got to lick the bowls! Her smoked mackerel pâté contains a fair amount of melted butter, but the oily mackerel is a healthy counter to it. I like it best served on toasted rye bread. She wrote out the recipe for me on the back of an envelope and miraculously I still have it. Her flowing round hand is unmistakable. Few of her written recipes survive, so I treasure this one.

Molly's Smoked Mackerel Pâté

SERVES 4–6
2 smoked mackerel (about 500g/1lb)
150g/5oz unsalted butter
2 pinches cayenne pepper
2 pinches ground mace or nutmeg
2 tbsp lemon juice
freshly milled salt and black pepper
watercress sprigs, to garnish
1 apple, sliced, to serve
lemon wedges, to serve

1 Remove the skin and bones from the fish and place in a food processor.

2 Melt the butter but don't let it brown and pour into the food processor. Blend until smooth.

3 Turn the mixture into a bowl, work in the cayenne pepper, mace or nutmeg and lemon juice. Add salt and pepper, taste and add more if needed.

4 Pack into a mould and garnish with the watercress. Serve with apple slices to cut the richness of the pâté and lemon wedges.

Vegetables

Sonia Keizs, an English neighbour, has green fingers and grows wonderful vegetables all year round. She often arrives with a bunch of something picked that morning, bursting out of its newspaper wrapping and demanding to be cooked forthwith. That is what's so nice about cooking seasonally – the choice is often made for you. It's about what's there – what looks good on the stand.

Here, broad beans, asparagus, purple sprouting broccoli, spinach, courgettes (zucchini), green beans, tomatoes, etc., all have their seasons and the wheel seems to turn the moment you find yourself thinking, 'I've had it with broccoli for a while!' One simple rule for vegetables, as with fish – they must be fresh. Well, two rules – the other being cook them until just soft to the bite, which means you must test them, so easy-to-use kitchen tongs are an essential tool.

My favourite way to eat broccoli is steamed with fruity olive oil and seasoning over it, but for a change you could try this spicy version.

Spicy Broccoli

SERVES 4

500g/1lb broccoli, cut into short-
  stemmed florets
4–5 tbsp olive oil, depending on how
  juicy the lemons are
4 garlic cloves, peeled and chopped
1 tsp cumin seeds
2–3 small red chillies, cored, deseeded
  and chopped, or a medium fresh
  green one, cored, deseeded and sliced
juice of 2 lemons

1 Steam the broccoli until just tender, then plunge into a bowl of cold water, drain and set aside.

2 Heat the olive oil in a medium sauté pan and gently soften the garlic.

3 Add the cumin seeds and the chillies. After half a minute, add the lemon juice. Stir well and check the oil/lemon balance. Cook on for a couple of minutes to let the flavours meld.

4 Fold in the broccoli and turn it to reheat and soak up the sauce.

Many years ago I had lunch in a tiny workers' café in the centre of Florence – only open at midday. I watched the owner put down a plate of steaming broccoli – that was all there was on the plate – in front of a burly Italian and place a large jug of olive oil and salt and pepper beside it. The man poured on the oil, seasoned the irresistible plateful and ate it. That's simple eating. Of course, he may have had a veal chop after I left!

Broccoli – Florence-style

SERVES 4

500g/1lb broccoli, stems stripped of
  rough outer layer and cut into bite-
  size pieces, florets cut likewise
olive oil
salt and pepper
lemon quarters

1 Steam the broccoli until tender, but don't overcook it. Test it from time to time with the end of a sharp knife.

2 Transfer to a serving bowl and pour over some olive oil – be generous with it.

3 Season generously too, and turn it all over carefully.

4 Serve with a small jug of olive oil on the table for those who are never satisfied, and some lemon quarters.

What to do with Brussels sprouts? This is a tasty option and quickly done. I favour the smaller ones as they are sweeter. Delicious served with a traditional roast chicken or turkey, of course.

Brussels Sprouts with Shallots

SERVES 4
15g/½oz butter
1 tbsp olive oil
3 shallots, peeled and sliced
500g/1lb Brussels sprouts, outer leaves
  removed and halved
3 tbsp vegetable stock
salt and pepper

1 Melt the butter with the olive oil in a medium frying pan and gently sweat the shallots until soft.

2 Add the halved Brussels sprouts and turn with the shallots.

3 Cook for a couple of minutes before adding the stock. Turn again and season.

4 Cover and cook on a low heat until the sprouts are tender but not mushy. You want to retain some of their lovely green colour.

Iris Molotsky, our host on a recent trip to Washington, DC and a fine cook herself, gave me this simple recipe. The results are surprising. Scorched black on the outside, the sprouts retain a lovely green succulence on the inside. They are all the rage, it seems.

Blackened Brussels Sprouts

SERVES 4 AS A SIDE VEGETABLE
500g/1lb Brussels sprouts, outer
  parts trimmed
3 tbsp olive oil
salt and pepper
salmon fillets or roast chicken,
  to serve

1 Preheat the oven to 200°C/400°F/Gas Mark 6. Place the sprouts in a bowl and add the olive oil, salt and pepper. Turn over to allow the oil to coat the sprouts thoroughly.

2 Empty them onto an oiled sheet of foil and spread over a shallow oven tray. Place the tray on the middle shelf of the oven. Roast for 30–45 minutes, depending on their size, shaking the pan every 10 minutes to brown the sprouts evenly. Reduce the heat if necessary to prevent burning. They should be dark brown, almost black, when done, but with a tender green interior.

3 Adjust the seasoning if necessary. Serve immediately with salmon fillets or roast chicken.

Our friend Tari Mandair was cooking lunch and I watched him stir-fry some cabbage to go with the chicken. Here's the recipe so you can replicate this beautifully green dish (pictured on page 76). Tari likes to cook this a little ahead of time to let the flavours meld, then reheats just before eating.

Tari's Stir-Fried Cabbage with Peas

SERVES 4

swirl of olive oil in the pan
1 tsp cumin seeds
1 medium cabbage, outer leaves
  removed, quartered, de-stemmed
  and sliced fine
1 tsp turmeric
pinch of red chilli flakes
couple of bay leaves
salt and pepper
a couple of handfuls of frozen
  green peas
Comfort Lentils (page 186), to serve

1 Heat the olive oil in a large sauté pan. Add the cumin seeds, and fry them briefly until they colour a little.

2 Add the cabbage, and turn it over thoroughly in the oil. Add the remaining spices and season with salt and pepper. Stir-fry the mix over a highish heat for about 5 minutes. The cabbage will wilt but retain a bit of a bite! Tari says that if the heat is too low, it will steam the cabbage and make it taste like hospital food; also, the little charred flecks of brown that add to its deliciousness won't be picked up. But be careful not to burn it!

3 Add the peas and turn them over with the cabbage. Try serving it with the Comfort Lentils.

This is a sprightly accompaniment to pretty much anything.

Courgettes (Zucchini) with Garlic and Parsley

SERVES 4

500g/1lb courgettes (zucchini)
salt and freshly ground pepper
1 tbsp olive oil
1 tbsp chopped parsley
1 garlic clove, peeled and finely
  chopped

1 Top and tail the courgettes. Peel them, leaving stripes of green. Cut them to index-finger thickness. Lightly salt them and leave for a good hour in a colander/sieve so they lose their liquid. Shake well and dry with kitchen paper.

2 Heat the olive oil in a large frying pan. Fry the courgette rounds over a high heat so they colour lightly. Turn over with a pair of tongs or a spatula (depending on the amount of rounds you may have to repeat this).

3 Grind over lots of pepper. Throw over the parsley and garlic. Toss well. Turn down the heat to low, cover and cook for a few more minutes, being careful not to overcook them.

A cabbage once got the job of representing my head. In 1971, I played the foolish, arrogant, headstrong Earl of Essex in *Elizabeth R* opposite a formidable Glenda Jackson as Elizabeth. The young jackanapes got it into his head to start a rebellion against the Virgin Queen. He'd been her favourite for years and had been forgiven much but this she couldn't ignore. He found himself on Tower Green with a rendezvous with the headsman. The powers that be decided the most realistic way to replicate the sound of a head being chopped off was to lop a cabbage in half! I have only recently been able to eat them without getting nervous! Here, the abused cabbage is restored to its proper place – on the table.

Interesting Cabbage

SERVES 2
2 tbsp olive oil
1 garlic clove, peeled and sliced thinly
1 small onion, peeled and
  chopped small
1 small cabbage, halved vertically,
  cored and shredded thinly
10 juniper berries, squashed
salt and pepper

1 Heat the olive oil in a medium sauté pan. When hot, sauté the garlic until it starts to colour. Add the onion and stir-fry until the onion catches up with the garlic.

2 Add the cabbage and the juniper berries and turn all together thoroughly in the garlic, onion and oil mix. Cover the pan, lower the heat and cook for a further 10 minutes to soften the cabbage. Add a splash of water if the cabbage starts to catch. Be generous with the pepper and sprinkle some salt over.

These have been a favourite for years. They go well with spicy food and make an effective complement – and a nice colour contrast – to a simply cooked salmon fillet. The recipe is adapted from one in Madhur Jaffrey's BBC cookbook *Indian Cookery*.

Green Beans with Garlic and Black Mustard Seeds

SERVES 4
500g/1lb green beans, topped
4 tbsp olive oil
1 tbsp black mustard seeds
4 garlic cloves, peeled and very finely
  chopped
1 dried red chilli, deseeded and
  finely chopped
1 tsp salt
pepper

1 Cook the beans to just tender in plenty of lightly salted, boiling water. The fresher the beans, the quicker they cook. After 5 minutes, use tongs to whip one out of the water to test for doneness – test in this manner until you judge them ready. Plunge into a bowl of cold water to stop them cooking further. Drain.

2 When you are ready to continue cooking, heat the olive oil in a frying pan and add the mustard seeds. When they start to pop, add the garlic. Cook until it starts to turn light brown – be careful not to burn it; it won't take long. Add the chilli and stir. Add the beans and the salt.

3 Turn the heat to low and fold the beans over in the oil and spices. (You are heating through and infusing the beans with the flavours; 2–3 minutes should do it.) Add the pepper, stir and serve.

This is also a good way to cook spinach.

Swiss Chard Leaves in Garlicky Olive Oil

SERVES 4
1kg/2lb Swiss chard
4 tbsp olive oil
1 large garlic clove, peeled and crushed
salt

1 Cut the leaves away from the stalks of the chard. (There is a delicious gratin for the stalks on page 181.) Soak and rinse them well. Shake off as much of the water as you can.

2 Heat the olive oil in a large saucepan or sauté pan. Put in the garlic and brown it over a moderate heat, taking care it doesn't burn.

3 Remove the garlic, add all the chard leaves and some salt, turning the leaves in the garlicky oil. Cover the pan and cook gently until the chard has collapsed and is a tender silky-green marvel. Turn it over again and serve.

Simple and delicious, this combination creates its own sauce while it cooks.

Leeks in White Wine and Butter

SERVES 4
4 large leeks, just the white part, checked for residue, then cut into 5cm/2in pieces
salt and pepper
glass of white wine
3 tbsp water
50g/2oz butter

1 Place the leek pieces in a shallow pan. Season with salt and pepper.

2 Pour in the wine and water, then add the butter. Put on the lid and bring to a simmer. Cook over a low heat for about 20 minutes – the leeks should be beautifully tender.

Based on a recipe from Richard Olney's *Simple French Food*, this could serve as a vegetarian main course with some white beans or chickpeas (garbanzo beans). The slow initial cooking helps to caramelise the fennel lightly, so it's worth taking the time.

Slow-cooked Fennel with Garlic

SERVES 4

2 large or 4 medium fennel bulbs, tough outer part removed, cleaned up and quartered, or cut into eighths if the bulbs are very large
6 or more garlic cloves, unpeeled (hooray!)
3 tbsp olive oil
salt and pepper
6 tbsp water

1 Put the fennel and the garlic in a pan large enough to hold all the quarters in a single layer. Add the olive oil and a little salt.

2 Cook, uncovered, on a medium-low heat for 20 minutes, turning as the fennel colours. It should be nicely caramelised.

3 Add the water, cover the pan and cook slowly until the fennel is super tender – about 30–40 minutes. The quarters should hold their shape and be infused with a deliciously mild taste of garlic. Adjust the seasoning and serve.

This would make a good accompaniment to some slow-fried sausages.

Red Cabbage with Apple and Fresh Fruit Juices

SERVES 4 PLUS, DEPENDING ON SIZE OF CABBAGE

1 onion, chopped
1 tbsp olive oil
12 juniper berries, crushed
2 apples, peeled, cored and diced
1 stick celery, chopped
1 red cabbage, cored, quartered and sliced
juice of 2 oranges and 2 lemons
1 tbsp wine vinegar
salt and pepper

1 Sweat the onion in the olive oil in a large saucepan until it softens.

2 Add the juniper berries and mix in.

3 Stir in the apple, celery and cabbage. Stir well and keep turning over gently for 5 minutes.

4 When the cabbage is starting to wilt, add the citrus juices and wine vinegar. Add some salt and cover the pan.

5 Cook for about 25 minutes – the cabbage should be a pinky red and soft. Add pepper and salt if needed.

Vegetarian Dishes

These dishes are suitable as main courses for vegetarians and indeed we often eat them as a light supper. Something I've learnt from living here in France is the custom of eating more lightly in the evening. It makes sense not to overload the digestive system at the end of the day. Other veggie options are to be found in the Vegetables, Pasta, Light Lunches and Salads chapters. Some vegetarians eat fish – which makes them non-meat eaters in my book, rather than vegetarian – which makes cooking for mixed company less complicated.

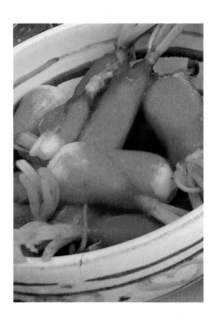

These aubergine (eggplant) halves, or boats, carry a simple cargo – homemade tomato sauce – and look beautiful as part of an al fresco summer lunch table.

Aubergine (Eggplant) Halves with Tomato Sauce

SERVES 2

2 aubergines (eggplant),
  halved lengthways
salt
olive oil
8 tbsp Quick Tomato Sauce
  (page 70)

1 Carefully, without piercing the skin, make two parallel diagonal slashes in the flesh side of the cut aubergines and repeat the process on the other side, as though you were going to play noughts and crosses! Sprinkle with a little salt and leave to drain in a colander for an hour.

2 Preheat the oven to 200°C/400°F/Gas Mark 6.

3 Pat the four halves dry with kitchen paper. Brush with olive oil and place on a shallow oven tray covered with lightly oiled foil. Place on the middle shelf of the oven and cook until tender – about 40 minutes; the time depends on the size of the aubergines, but they must be soft.

4 Take them out of the oven and spread a couple of generous tablespoons of the tomato sauce on the top of each half – more if necessary. Return to the oven for about 20 minutes. You can let them rest for 10 minutes before serving.

Jamie Oliver calls this traditional Sicilian wonder 'incredible Sicilian Aubergine Stew'. It's a good description. There are echoes of ratatouille, of course.

Caponata

SERVES 4

2 tbsp olive oil, plus extra to serve

2 large aubergines (eggplant), cut in chunks, salted and left to drain, overnight if you can but at least an hour or two (they will soak up less oil when cooked)

1 tsp dried oregano

1 small red onion, peeled and finely chopped

2 garlic cloves, peeled and finely sliced

1 small bunch parsley, stalks chopped separately very finely (also chop the leaves finely to scatter over the finished dish)

a handful of green olives, pitted if you have time

2 tbsp capers

2–3 tbsp herb vinegar (I use tarragon vinegar), not more or it dominates

5 ripe tomatoes (or tinned if it's not the season), roughly chopped

salt and pepper

1 Heat the olive oil in a large pan. Give the aubergines a squeeze, dry them thoroughly and add to the pan with the oregano. Cook on the highest heat to brown the chunks, turning them as they colour. This is the longest part of the cooking, as you may have to do this in a couple of stages.

2 When the aubergines are nicely coloured, add the onion, garlic and the parsley stalks. Cook for a couple of minutes. Add a little more olive oil if you feel it needs it.

3 Add the olives, capers and herb vinegar.

4 When the vinegar has evaporated, add the tomatoes, bring back to a simmer and cook for 15–20 minutes until the aubergines are really melting.

5 Season with pepper and salt, bearing in mind that you salted the aubergines earlier.

6 Sprinkle over the parsley leaves. Serve with extra olive oil to hand.

After a night that registered -10°C, a bowl of something gently spicy and soupy for lunch was just the ticket – a quick excursion to the East. Rose Elliot found this in Julie Sahni's *Classic Indian Vegetarian Cookery* and adapted it. I have tweaked it a bit. There was a small cabbage in the fridge and some fenugreek seeds in the larder, which I whizzed into powder in a converted coffee grinder. (The fenugreek is optional but interesting. As its name implies, this herb is found in the Mediterranean region; it has healing qualities as well as culinary uses.)

Cabbage and Red Lentils

SERVES 4

250g/8oz red lentils
1.3 litres/2¼ pints stock
⅓ tsp turmeric
375g/12oz tinned tomatoes, chopped
1 tbsp olive oil
1½ tsp black mustard seeds
1 tbsp curry powder
¼ tsp fenugreek powder (optional)
1 onion, peeled and chopped
1 small cabbage, outer leaves removed,
   quartered, cored and shredded
salt and pepper
juice of ½ lemon
parsley, or even better still, fresh
   coriander (cilantro), chopped to
   sprinkle over

1 Rinse the lentils thoroughly. Put them in a saucepan with the stock and the turmeric and bring to the boil. Cook at a gentle simmer for 15–20 minutes, stirring a couple of times.

2 Add the chopped tomatoes then set aside.

3 Heat the olive oil in a different pan. Add the mustard seeds and cook them until they start to pop – a couple of minutes.

4 Mix in the curry powder and the fenugreek (if using) and let them cook for a few seconds. Add the onion and the cabbage and mix everything together well. Cover the pan and cook for 5 minutes.

5 Add the wilted cabbage to the lentils. Bring the mixture to a simmer, and leave to simmer gently for 20 minutes.

6 Season to taste with salt and pepper. Stir in the lemon juice. Sprinkle over the parsley or coriander. It's best served hot.

The other night I was looking for something easy to cook, preferably in a single pot; a ladleful of taste over some brown basmati rice – comfort food that cooks itself. I looked in the fridge and, as happens regularly, found a cauliflower (in good condition!) and a leek, and a bottle of chickpeas (garbanzo beans) on the shelf in the larder. I knew there were a few small tomatoes left to gather at the end of the garden – perfect!

Cauliflower, Leek and Chickpea (Garbanzo Bean) Curry

SERVES 3–4

1 onion, peeled and chopped small
2 garlic cloves, peeled and chopped
2 tbsp olive oil
1 tsp black mustard seeds
1 tsp each turmeric, cumin powder, ginger powder
½ tsp each coriander powder, cayenne powder
250g/8oz tomatoes, chopped roughly
salt and pepper
600ml/1 pint stock
1 leek, cleaned and sliced
1 cauliflower, separated into bite-size florets
3 tbsp bottled or tinned chickpeas, drained and rinsed
2 tbsp whisked yogurt or coconut cream, unsweetened and with the consistency of milk
cooked brown basmati rice, to serve

1 In a large pan, sweat the onion and garlic in the olive oil, uncovered, until softened and beginning to colour.

2 Add the mustard seeds and let them cook for a minute. Add the rest of the spices and mix them in.

3 Add the tomatoes, stirring them into the spice mix and season with salt and pepper. Cook for 5 minutes to break them down a little and form a sauce.

4 Add half the stock and cook for a further 5 minutes, reducing it a little.

5 Mix in the leeks and cauliflower – you may find you only need half the head – making sure the vegetables are immersed in the liquid.

6 Cook on a low heat for 30 minutes, checking now and then in case it's drying up, as it very nearly did for me! Add more stock as you need and continue to cook.

7 Add the chickpeas and cook for a further 5 minutes.

8 When the vegetables are tender, turn off the heat and let it cool down. Fold in the yogurt or coconut cream. Gently reheat to serve over some brown basmati rice.

This is based on a *River Cafe Cook Book* recipe and is a handy dish as a vegetarian main course – but lovely with grilled or fried sausages too!

Chickpeas (Garbanzo Beans) with Tomato Sauce and Spinach

SERVES 6–8

2 tbsp Quick Tomato Sauce (page 70)
5 tbsp olive oil
1 fennel bulb, chopped into small dice
1 red onion, peeled and chopped small
large stick of celery, chopped into
    small dice
2 dried chillies
salt and pepper
250ml/9 fl oz white wine
900g/32oz tinned chickpeas (garbanzo
    beans), drained and rinsed
500g/1lb spinach or Swiss chard leaves,
    thoroughly washed and
    spun dry
3 tbsp chopped parsley
more olive oil
juice of ½ lemon

1 Make the tomato sauce.

2 Heat the olive oil in a large sauté pan. Add the fennel, onion and celery, and soften for about 20 minutes.

3 Add the chillies and season well.

4 Add the wine and reduce down until just the oil remains.

5 Add the tomato sauce and cook gently for 10 minutes.

6 Add the chickpeas and the spinach or Swiss chard leaves, and turn in carefully. You can add the spinach in handfuls – covering the pan for a minute each time; it will spill but it's satisfying to see it gradually wilt and become part of the dish when it's thoroughly heated through.

7 Fold in the parsley, sprinkle over a little more olive oil and the lemon juice.

This is adapted from Jojo Tulloh's *Freshly Picked – Kitchen Garden Cooking in the City* and is handy for vegetarians – when others are having fishcakes, perhaps. It's important to check the seasoning for depth, as you assemble the mixture. Tzatziki (page 68) on the side is recommended.

Courgette (Zucchini) Fritters

SERVES 2–3

3 medium courgettes (zucchini), scrubbed and dried
salt and pepper
2 large-bulbed spring onions, cleaned and grated
1 garlic clove, peeled and finely chopped
zest of 1 lemon
1 tbsp chickpea (garbanzo bean) flour
1 tbsp chopped herbs, e.g. mint, parsley, chives
2 eggs, beaten
2 tbsp olive oil

1 Grate the courgettes into a colander. Salt them lightly and leave for at least an hour to drain. Squeeze out the remaining liquid. It's important to take the time for this, especially when the courgettes are young and fresh, otherwise the mixture will be too watery.

2 Put the rest of the ingredients, except the eggs and the olive oil, in a mixing bowl and add the courgettes. Season well, bearing in mind you have already salted the courgettes. Combine everything thoroughly, then check the seasoning.

3 Add the whisked eggs and mix in.

4 Heat a tablespoon of olive oil in a large frying pan. Scoop up a dessertspoonful of the mixture and drop it into the pan. Press it down with the flat of the spoon. Repeat the process but don't overcrowd the pan.

5 Cook over a medium-hot heat quite quickly but be careful not to burn the fritters. Take a peek with a spatula, then flip them over after a couple of minutes. Check they are cooked through and serve.

Our friend Helen Richmond is an insouciant cook, a quality I have yet to achieve. She will throw some of this and a little more of that into her tall saucepan and very quickly the aroma of a delicious lunch fills her kitchen. A neighbour's gift of a large cauliflower sat on her counter begging for attention one morning we were there. Helen made a sauce of olive oil, paprika and lemon juice to bathe it in before roasting it in a moderate oven for 40-odd minutes. She served it with slices of pork fillet roasted with rosemary from her garden. The dish turned out to be one of those you find yourself sneaking back to when the hostess isn't looking. *Ju-ust* one more little piece . . . ! Helen is happy for me to reproduce the recipe here.

Helen's Spicy Cauliflower

SERVES 3–4

2 tbsp olive oil

1 tsp paprika, sweet smoked if you have any to hand

juice of ½ lemon, plus a little extra water (I noticed Helen fill the squeezed lemon halves with water and squeeze them out again, getting the most out of a lemon!)

1 cauliflower, stem removed and split into smallish florets

salt and pepper

1 Preheat the oven to 160°C/325°F/Gas Mark 3. In a large bowl, whisk the olive oil, paprika and lemon juice together to form a dark red viscous sauce.

2 Add the cauliflower florets to the bowl and turn them over and over in the sauce. Sprinkle with salt and pepper.

3 Spread them out on a shallow roasting tray. Roast in the centre of the oven for about 40 minutes.

This is a useful and reliable dish – served as a starter or a light lunch with a green salad. A single half-pepper may be enough to serve per person as a starter.

Red Peppers Stuffed with Tomato and Chèvre

SERVES 4

4 red peppers, choose ones that will balance well when halved
8 medium ripe fresh tomatoes or tinned ones, quartered
4 garlic cloves, peeled and finely sliced
2 round fresh chèvres (goats' cheese), as fresh as you can find, cut in half
8 tbsp olive oil, plus extra for brushing
salt and pepper
8 basil leaves (optional but nice)

1 Preheat the oven to 200°C/400°F/Gas Mark 6.

2 Cut the peppers in half lengthways through the stem, and cut out the white stem base and remove the seeds.

3 Put a quartered tomato and some sliced garlic in each half-pepper. Tuck half a chèvre in each. Drizzle a tablespoon of olive oil over each half and season with salt and pepper.

4 Cover a shallow oven pan with foil and brush it with oil. Place the pepper halves carefully on the pan, cook them in the upper part of the oven for about 40 minutes–1 hour; the time depends on the size and thickness of the peppers, but they should be very tender and oozing with the sweet juices of the tomatoes and peppers when you check for doneness after about 30 minutes.

5 Put a basil leaf on each. They are best served warm, not too hot.

Adapted from Rose Elliot's *The Bean Book*, this is a simple solution for people who don't eat meat but like the look of chilli – leave out the *carne*! After experimenting with variations – the addition of cumin powder and even Dijon mustard – I settled for *the simpler the better*. Quickly done, it tastes even nicer the next day. Don't forget the lemon!

Red Bean Chilli

SERVES 2–3

1 onion, peeled and chopped
1 garlic clove, peeled and chopped
2 tbsp olive oil
1 tsp chilli or cayenne powder
1 x 400g/13oz tin tomatoes, chopped, with all the juice
500g/1lb red kidney beans (from a jar or tin)
salt and pepper
juice of ½ lemon or more, to taste
cooked brown basmati rice and Cumin Yogurt Sauce (page 68), to serve

1 Soften the onion and garlic gently in the olive oil in a medium casserole or saucepan, stirring often.

2 Add the chilli or cayenne powder and the chopped tomatoes with their juice. Mix these all together, blending in the tomatoes.

3 Add the beans and season with salt and pepper. Bring gently to a simmer and cook, covered, for 15 minutes.

4 Pour over the lemon juice and mix in.

5 Serve over some brown basmati rice with perhaps a bowl of the Cumin Yogurt Sauce.

Adapted from Delia Smith's recipe, this is useful as a starter or light main course. It also looks good in summer served with the salmon fillet on page 116 with some green beans.

Roast Ratatouille

SERVES 4

500g/1lb cherry tomatoes, vary the colour if you see them

2 courgettes (zucchini), cut into 2.5cm/1in dice

1 aubergine (eggplant), cut roughly the same as the courgettes

2 yellow or red peppers, deseeded and cut as above

1 red onion, peeled and chopped as above

2 large garlic cloves, peeled and finely chopped

3 tbsp olive oil and extra for brushing

some basil leaves

salt and pepper

Tapenade (page 73) and cubed feta cheese, to serve

1 Preheat the oven to its hottest – i.e. 240°C/475°F/Gas Mark 9.

2 Put all the vegetables in a large bowl, sprinkle over the garlic, mix in the olive oil and the basil. Season with salt and pepper and turn it all over thoroughly.

3 Fold all this carefully onto a large shallow roasting tin that you have already brushed with oil or covered in oiled foil. Space so that the vegetables have room to catch the heat otherwise they will stew.

4 Place the tin on the highest rack of the oven. Roast for 20 minutes – check after 10 minutes for burning and 'doneness' ('charred' is good, 'burned' not so good!); roasting time will vary depending on the thickness of the vegetables and your oven.

5 Serve Tapenade sauce with this if you like – it goes particularly well; and you could try adding some cubes of feta cheese for the last 10 minutes – thus calling in at various spots on the Mediterranean!

It seems a contradiction in terms – they are called *sweet* potatoes, after all – but this vegetable is fine for diabetics; it has a different fibre make-up from the ordinary potato and a lower GI rating. It's delicious too!

Baked Sweet Potato with Fillings

SERVES 4

2 medium-size sweet potatoes, evenly shaped; of course, you could also cook one per person

1 Preheat the oven to 190°C/375°F/Gas Mark 5.

2 Lightly score a circle lengthways round the middle of the potatoes with the point of a sharp knife, just breaking the skin. This is to stop them bursting in the heat.

3 Place them high in the oven and cook for about an hour or until tender when pierced through. Remove from the oven, halve lengthways and fill.

POSSIBLE FILLINGS

• Simple seasoning: salt and pepper – and olive oil.

• A yogurt of choice. (See method for making it thicker, on page 216.) Depotting the yogurt and whisking it first makes it more agreeable to eat. You can add a little crushed garlic to it and/or some cumin powder – or whatever you like, of course.

• Gently sautéed diced bacon goes well – smoked or unsmoked.

• The broccoli and anchovy sauce (page 158) is also good – it's your choice!

…this vegetable is
fine for diabetics.
It's *delicious* too!

Fish and Seafood

Fish is not to everyone's taste—'too many bones', 'the heads put me off', 'how do you cook it?' The recipes here are not complicated and may help to persuade the unconverted to have second thoughts. Fish has to be super fresh – a mushy mackerel is a waste of time and will put people off eating fish, as overcooked cabbage and broccoli put generations of school kids off vegetables. If it is fresh, it needs very little help – there are two or three simple sauces in this section that complement rather than mask and are worth offering up.

This recipe is adapted from *Marcella's Kitchen* (Marcella Hazan, of course), a book well worth seeking out. It makes a good lunch or light supper. A plate of green beans, dressed with olive oil and salt and/or some lovely ripe tomatoes, sliced and similarly dressed, would go beautifully with this very tasty dish.

Baked Mackerel Fillets

SERVES 4

4 mackerel fillets, very fresh (essential with mackerel), skin and small bones removed (ask your fishmonger to do this)

STUFFING

3 tbsp olive oil and extra for brushing
5 tbsp wholewheat breadcrumbs
3 tbsp chopped parsley
1 garlic clove, peeled and chopped
3 anchovy fillets, chopped
3 tbsp capers, chopped
salt and pepper
tomato salad, to serve

1 Preheat the oven to 200°C/400°F/Gas Mark 6.

2 Reserve one tablespoon each of the olive oil and breadcrumbs. Mix together thoroughly with the remaining stuffing ingredients in a bowl.

3 Wash and pat the fish dry, removing any lingering bones.

4 Line a shallow baking tray with some foil and brush with oil to prevent the fillets sticking. Lay half the fillets skin side down and spoon over half the stuffing. Cover each with a second fillet and spoon over what's left of the stuffing. Sprinkle with the remaining breadcrumbs and olive oil (add more oil if you think it needs it).

5 Bake in the top of the oven for 15 minutes or more, depending on the thickness of the fillets. They should come out sizzling and the breadcrumbs crispy on top – but be careful not to overcook them.

6 A ripe tomato salad is a good counter to the richness of the mackerel.

A very good dish to serve guests, this recipe is easily adapted to feed more than four. Allow 200g/7oz of salmon fillet per person.

Blackened Salmon with Orange Yogurt Sauce

SERVES 4

800g/28oz salmon fillet, skin and small
   bones removed
2 tbsp olive oil, plus extra for sautéing
cooked brown basmati rice, to serve

FOR THE ORANGE YOGURT SAUCE

4 tbsp olive oil
400ml/14 fl oz yogurt of choice,
   whisked smooth
zest and juice of 1 large juicy orange

FOR THE HERB AND SPICE MIX

3 tsp each dried thyme, dried rosemary,
   dried oregano
3 tsp dry-roasted cumin seeds,
   roughly ground
1½ tsp each Spanish sweet smoked
   paprika, cayenne pepper
3 garlic cloves, peeled and pulped in
   a mortar with a pinch of salt
3 tsp salt, ground fine if sea salt

1 Make the sauce by whisking the olive oil into the yogurt, followed by the zest and juice of the orange. Set aside.

2 Put all the herbs and spices in a bowl and mix them thoroughly.

3 Run your fingers over the top of the salmon fillets to check that all the small bones have been removed. Cut the salmon into squares roughly 3cm/1½in in size – they need to be cooked quite quickly so mustn't be too large. Put them in a bowl and add the olive oil. Turn the salmon pieces carefully until well covered.

4 Tip the salmon into the bowl with the herb and spice mix. Again, turn the salmon carefully until all the pieces are well coated in the mix.

5 Pour a couple of tablespoons of olive oil into a large frying pan. When hot, transfer the 'blackened' salmon to the pan and fry for 4–5 minutes, turning to cook evenly. Check for doneness, trying not to overcook; it's better that some pieces are slightly underdone – they continue to cook a bit off the heat.

6 Serve over a steaming dish of brown basmati rice. Don't forget the sauce on the side!

Simon Hopkinson uses butter and vermouth in this simple recipe from his book, *The Good Cook*. I'm trying it with olive oil and white wine, which fits in better with our way of eating. The single pot and the short cooking time make it a useful quick lunch. The timings can vary depending on the thickness of the salmon fillets.

Salmon Fillets Baked in Spinach

SERVES 2

2 tbsp olive oil

1 shallot, peeled and finely chopped

2 tbsp white wine

300g/10oz spinach, washed, de-spined and spun free of water

2 salmon fillets, skin left on

salt and pepper

grating of nutmeg

1 Heat a tablespoon of olive oil in a medium pan with a lid. Sauté the chopped shallot for a couple of minutes to soften it. Add the wine and leave it to bubble for a moment or two.

2 Lay a third of the spinach in the pan and place the salmon fillets over it. Sprinkle over some salt and pepper and a grating of nutmeg. Cover the salmon with the rest of the spinach. Scatter the remaining tablespoon of oil over the spinach and cover the pan. Cook for 7 minutes over a low heat.

3 Turn the heat off and leave the pan covered for 10 minutes before serving.

'No oil?' is the most frequently asked question when I suggest this miraculously simple and effective recipe. Yes – no oil and a cold pan on the lowest heat. A little patience comes in handy, though! The other night we had these salmon fillets with basmati brown rice, green beans sprinkled with olive oil and the Green Sauce on page 72.

Simple Salmon Fillet (1)

SERVES 4
4 fillets of salmon, skin left on and
    weighing about 180–200g/6–7oz each
salt and pepper

1 Run your finger over the surface of the fillets to check for bones. Wash the fillets and pat dry. Place them in a sauté pan skin side down.

2 Without any oil added to the pan, cook them over the lowest possible heat for about 20 minutes, or until you see the lower half becoming opaque.

3 Season with salt and pepper and cover the pan. Continue cooking until a creamy white juice forms on the surface of the fillets, indicating that they are done. The whole process can take 30 minutes, depending on the thickness of the fillets – it's the slow cooking that produces the wonderful result.

I include this because it is easy and quick to do for company – a fillet a person. Swiss chard or spinach goes well and lends a lovely contrast in colour.

Simple Salmon Fillet (2)

SERVES AS MANY PEOPLE AS
YOU HAVE FILLETS!
Fillets of salmon, skin left on,
    checked for bones, washed and
    patted dry
oil
salt and pepper
lemon wedges, to serve

1 Preheat the oven to 140°C/275°F/Gas Mark 1.

2 Cover the bottom of a shallow roasting tin with foil and oil it lightly. Place the fillets on top. Salt and pepper them. Cook on the middle shelf of the oven for 15 minutes – as for the previous recipe, the white juices indicate doneness.

3 Serve with lemon wedges.

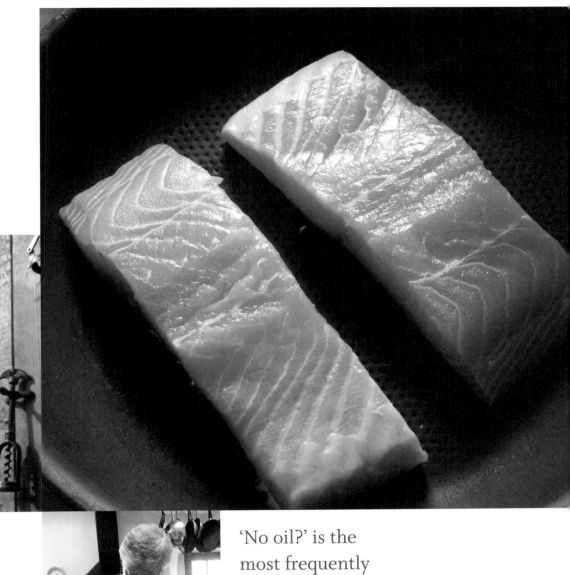

'No oil?' is the most frequently asked question when I suggest this miraculously simple and effective recipe.

This is adapted from Nigel Slater's recipe. It's a good dish for company – allow 150g/5oz fish per person. You can make the basic sauce earlier or even the night before and prepare the fish pieces too. Then all you have to do is reheat the curry sauce and slip in the fish in the appropriate order while you cook some basmati rice. Can also be served with cucumber raita or a fresh chutney.

Fish Curry

SERVES 4

2 medium onions, peeled and chopped
2 garlic cloves, peeled and chopped
1 tbsp olive oil
1 tsp black mustard seeds
thumbnail-size piece of fresh ginger, chopped
3 small red chillies (the heat level is a matter of taste), cored, deseeded and chopped
1 tsp each garam masala (page 215), cayenne (less if you prefer), turmeric
250g/8oz fresh or tinned tomatoes, chopped
600ml/1 pint stock
250g/8oz mussels
8 clams, if you can find them
600g/21oz white fish in fillets: monkfish, haddock, cod or some of each, preferably fish that holds its shape when cooked in pieces
8 prawns in their shells
1 tbsp yogurt, whisked smooth
salt
a handful of chopped parsley

1 In a casserole large enough to hold all the fish, fry the onions and garlic gently in the olive oil until soft.

2 Add the mustard seeds and ginger and mix.

3 Add the chopped chilli and mix.

4 Add the garam masala, cayenne and turmeric and mix.

5 Add the chopped tomatoes and let them mingle with the spices for 5 minutes.

6 Add the stock and bring everything to the boil.

7 Let this sauce simmer for 15 minutes.

8 Clean the mussels (i.e. remove the beards and scrape free of any gunge). Scrub the clams if you have them. Check the fish fillets for bones and cut into bite-size pieces. Have the prawns standing by.

9 Stir in the yogurt carefully. Reheat the sauce if you have precooked it.

10 Slip in the white fish and cook until it turns opaque – about 5 minutes.

11 Then add the mussels, clams and prawns. Bring them back to a strong simmer and cook gently, making sure the sauce is covering the fish, until the mussels and clams open and the prawns heat through. (I sometimes throw the mussels and clams in a saucepan with a tablespoon of water to get them to open, then add them to the curry.)

12 Check the salt, add the parsley and bring this bubbling colourful wonder to the table.

Another recipe based on a Nigel Slater recipe. I have always loved fishcakes – must be the comfort food factor kicking in – but these days of course, the fact they usually contain 50 per cent potato causes trouble for me as a diabetic. This recipe solves the problem! The dill and the grain mustard make the fishcakes special and they sometimes serve as a tasty starter. If you keep them small and cook them quickly, they'll be crisp and brown on the outside and still succulent inside.

Salmon Fishcakes

SERVES 2

YOGURT SAUCE
2 x 125g/4oz pots yogurt
1 tsp grain mustard
good pinch of chopped dill
  (from the main bunch)
salt

THE FISHCAKES
500g/1lb salmon fillet, skinless and
  checked for bones
white of 1 egg
1 tbsp chickpea (garbanzo bean) flour,
  of course plain flour works as well
1 tsp grain mustard
juice of ½ lemon
bunch of dill, finely chopped
salt and pepper
2 tbsp olive oil
Fennel Salad (page 55), to serve

1 Mix together all the Yogurt Sauce ingredients and refrigerate until you are ready to eat.

2 Cut up the salmon fillets into roughly equal-size pieces. Put these in a food processor and pulse three or four times. Avoid working them too much and producing a slush. You could just cut them up into small pieces if you prefer.

3 Put the salmon in a bowl. Turn in the egg white and the flour, and then the mustard, lemon juice and the dill. Season with salt and pepper.

4 It's a good idea to taste the mix for seasoning at this point – the dill and the salt should come through.

5 Refrigerate if not using immediately.

6 Heat the olive oil in a frying pan and using a dessertspoon, scoop out a dollop and make a ball. Put this in the pan and flatten it gently. Cook on a medium-high flame for a couple of minutes each side, crisping and browning the outside while making sure the interior cooks through.

7 Serve with a Fennel Salad and the mustardy yogurt dipping sauce on the side.

This is based on a recipe by Marcella Hazan and is a regular lunch dish here. It's simple and satisfying. The best mussels are called *bouchot*. The word describes the method of cultivation – i.e. on a pole stuck in the estuary. They are not huge but are *plein* (full) and yellow when cooked. The amount of mussels I recommend using in this recipe is generous and will probably serve 6, but they are delicious, so who knows?

Spicy Mussels with a Soupy Sauce

SERVES 4

2 large garlic cloves, peeled
  and chopped
6 tbsp olive oil
2 tbsp chopped parsley
2–3 dry chillies, to taste, deseeded
  and chopped
300g/12oz tinned (or fresh) tomatoes,
  drained and chopped
2kg/4lb mussels, cleaned
  (i.e. beardless and scraped free
  of any gunge)
4 slices of wholewheat bread
1 garlic clove

1 In a large casserole, sauté the garlic in the oil until it colours.

2 Add the parsley and chillies. Stir a couple of times.

3 Add the tomatoes. Cook for about 25 minutes over a moderate heat, stirring from time to time.

4 When the sauce is ready, put in the mussels and turn them over carefully in it. Cover and turn up the heat to high. Give the casserole a shake, gripping the top with your thumbs, or stir the mussels again in the sauce. They will take about 5 minutes to cook through. They are ready when they have opened up well.

5 Toast the bread and rub with the bruised garlic clove. Pile the steaming mussels on top of the toast to serve.

As always, use very fresh fish. You can make the sauce beforehand and add the fish 10 minutes before serving. This dish is very comforting on a rainy day. Swiss chard or spinach goes well with it or you could simply serve rice.

Fish in Tomato and White Wine Sauce

SERVES 4

4 tbsp olive oil
1 small onion, peeled and chopped
2 garlic cloves, peeled and chopped
2 tbsp chopped parsley
8 tbsp white wine
200g/7oz tinned tomatoes and their juice, broken up
salt and pepper
1kg/2lb white fish fillet – hake, haddock, cod are good choices – washed and patted dry

1 To make the sauce, heat the olive oil in a pan large enough to take all the fish in a single layer. Add the onion and garlic, and cook gently until the onion is soft and the garlic begins to colour.

2 Add the parsley and stir in.

3 Turn up the heat and add the wine – let it bubble for a minute or so. Add the tomatoes and fold in.

4 Turn the heat down and, stirring occasionally, cook gently for 20 minutes. Season and taste.

5 When you are ready to use it, bring the sauce up to simmer and season the fish. Add to the sauce and cook gently for 5 minutes.

6 Turn over carefully and cook for a further 5 minutes.

This dish, and the Simple Salmon Fillet (1) (page 116), are based on recipes from an article I cut out from a newspaper ages ago by Quentin Blake, the illustrator. You can cook sea bream in the same way, though you might need two to make up the weight, and these won't need to be cooked as long – perhaps 15–20 minutes. I recently used rosemary instead of thyme, which worked well.

Simple Sea Bass

SERVES 4
1 x 1.25kg/2½lb bass, scales left on
salt and pepper
large bunch thyme, broken into sprigs
green beans, Courgettes (Zucchini)
   with Garlic and Parsley (page 81) or
   green salad, to serve
Simple Sauce (page 73), to serve

1 Preheat the oven to 240°C/475°F/Gas Mark 9.

2 Wash and dry the fish, being careful not to remove the scales. Salt the inside and stuff with sprigs of thyme.

3 Lay the fish on the remaining thyme in an oven tray and add salt and pepper. Cook for 25 minutes, adjusting the time to suit the fish as necessary.

4 Peel back the hardened skin to release the beautifully cooked fillets. This is a bit tricky but worth taking time over.

5 Serve with green beans and Courgettes (Zucchini) with Garlic and Parsley, or a green salad and Simple Sauce.

Poultry

Chicken is versatile – it is readily available, the ways to cook it are legion, and it is reasonably priced. It is also a healthy option and, as Jamie Oliver says of his way of roasting, it is simply delicious. Guinea fowl and quail are easy to find now and fun to try too. Where we live, quail are farmed and readily available. They are a fair size too, so one or one and a half per person is enough. Both quail and guinea fowl have a hint of game about them, which makes it a good choice for company as a change from chicken. Guinea fowl with cider, fennel and apples is a favourite dish of mine – both comforting and elegant.

Our friend Charlotte Fraser – a wonderful cook and co-author of *Flavours of the Sun* – put me on to this and it has been very useful. It's spicy and delicious and a good dish for company because it gently gets on with cooking itself, and needs only rice as an accompaniment.

Charlotte's Chicken Tagine

SERVES 4

1 free-range/organic chicken, weighing about 2kg/4.5lb, jointed into 8–10 pieces
3 onions, peeled and cut into eighths
2 medium fennel bulbs, outer leaves cut off, cored and cut into eighths
6 garlic cloves, peeled and chopped
1 tsp each turmeric, cumin, paprika, cayenne, ground ginger
1 tsp saffron threads
salt and pepper
240ml/8 fl oz vegetable stock
olive oil
a good handful of green olives
1 preserved lemon, zest only, cut in strips
2 tbsp chopped coriander (cilantro) or parsley
cooked brown basmati rice, to serve

1 Put the chicken pieces in a casserole or, even better, a tagine if you have one.

2 Scatter over the onion and fennel.

3 Sprinkle over the garlic and all the spices. Season with salt and pepper.

4 Pour over the stock and drizzle over some olive oil.

5 Turn everything over with care and gently bring to the boil – about 15 minutes. Put the lid on and cook at a gentle simmer for about 40 minutes, basting occasionally. The chicken pieces should be sumptuously melted and collapsed and the vegetables tender when ready.

6 Add the olives and lemon zest and continue cooking for 10–15 minutes.

7 Add the coriander or parsley just before serving with a steaming plate of brown basmati rice.

…a good dish for company because it gently gets on with cooking itself.

This makes a lazy supper or lunch and is no less delicious for that. The trick, if you can call it that, is to cook the chicken very gently – then it doesn't dry out. Sautéed spinach or Swiss chard goes well with this and perhaps half a baked sweet potato – the colour scheme is inviting.

Chicken Breasts with a Caper and Lemony Sauce

SERVES 4

4 free-range/organic chicken breasts
2 tbsp flour – I use chickpea (garbanzo bean) – seasoned with salt and pepper
4 tbsp olive oil or 50g/2oz butter – I prefer oil
1 lemon, zest and juice
2 tbsp capers, chopped

1 Drag the chicken pieces in the well-seasoned flour, pressing them down so they get a good dusting. Shake off the excess.

2 Heat the olive oil or butter in a medium frying pan – large enough to hold the chicken in one layer. When hot, slip in the chicken breasts. Turn the heat to low and cook for 15 minutes or so, turning them once or twice, until just past the pink stage; you can cut carefully into the thickest part of the chicken to test. Transfer the chicken to warm plates using a slotted spoon.

3 Add the lemon juice, zest and capers to the pan and season. Cook gently for a minute, stir and taste for perfection. Spoon some sauce over each serving of chicken.

This makes a lazy
supper or lunch and
is no less delicious
for that.

Based on one of Anna Del Conte's recipes, which I must have used 50 times! It's simple and good for small company. We are lucky to have wonderful fat quail farmed near here. Serve over chickpea (garbanzo bean) mash (see page 193).

Quail Roasted in Balsamic Vinegar

SERVES 4
8 quail, heads off and washed
  and dried
salt and pepper
olive oil
100ml/3½ fl oz stock
3 tbsp balsamic vinegar
30g/1oz butter

1 Preheat the oven to 200°C/400°F/Gas Mark 6.

2 Season the quail thoroughly with salt and pepper.

3 Heat some oil in an ovenproof pan and brown the quail on all sides.

4 Drizzle 2–3 tablespoons of stock over the birds and put them in the oven. They will take between 15–25 minutes to cook, depending on size. Baste them a couple of times and halfway through drizzle a couple of tablespoons of the balsamic vinegar over them.

5 Test for doneness by gently pulling a leg away from the body: it should come away easily and the flesh be turning from pink to light brown.

6 Park the quail in a warm dish and deglaze the pan with the remaining balsamic over a gentle heat. Add a couple more tablespoons of stock to the pan and reduce the liquid a little. Add the butter in small pieces and stir in well. Pour some of this over the quail and the rest into a serving jug.

This is a tasty Eastern take on gently sautéed chicken breasts. Serve with seasonal vegetables such as broccoli in winter or green beans in summer.

Chicken Breasts in a Spicy Lemon and Parsley Sauce

SERVES 4

1 largish onion, peeled and chopped
1 cinnamon stick, broken up
4 tbsp olive oil
4 free range/organic chicken breasts, spliced in half lengthways
juice of 2 lemons
salt and pepper
2 tbsp parsley, chopped
2–3 small red chillies, cored, deseeded and chopped

1 Cook the onion with the cinnamon gently in the oil until soft.

2 Add the chicken breasts with the lemon juice, and season with salt and pepper. Turn them over after 3 minutes and cook for a further 3 minutes.

3 Add the parsley and the chillies. Turn the chicken breasts in the sauce and continue cooking for a further 5 minutes. The exact cooking time depends on the thickness of the breasts. Cut into the thickest part of one to check: if it is still very pink, continue to cook for another couple of minutes.

Every cook has a version of this classic. This one is based on Jamie Oliver's simple, tasty and robust recipe. Serve with the Green Sauce (page 72) or Chimichurri (page 69).

Delicious Roast Chicken

SERVES 4
olive oil
1 free-range/organic chicken
    weighing about 1.5kg/3lb
salt and pepper
6 bay leaves
3 garlic cloves, unpeeled and whole
1 lemon, halved
1 glass white wine

1 Preheat the oven to 190°C/375°F/Gas Mark 5.

2 Rub the olive oil all over the chicken and season well. Stuff the cavity with the bay leaves, garlic and lemon halves.

3 Roast the chicken for 1½ hours. Halfway through, take it out of the oven and baste. When it is cooked, the chicken should be nicely browned and the juices clear, not pink.

4 Take the pan out of the oven. Tip it carefully and spoon out the excess fat/oil, leaving a spoonful in the pan. Pick up the bird with a pair of oven gloves and up-end it, letting the juices run back into the pan. This is a little tricky but worth it for the flavour it adds to the gravy. Park the chicken on a warmed (if possible) serving plate and leave it to rest covered in foil while you make the gravy.

5 Add the glass of white wine to the pan and scrape out any residue sticking to the bottom. Transfer to the hob and gently stir over a lowish heat for 2–3 minutes. You can add some stock or more wine to make it go a little further. Taste and pour into a warmed jug.

Our friend and neighbour Julie Ide put me onto this recipe, which originated from food writer Josceline Dimbleby. The anti-inflammatory and antioxidant qualities of the spices turmeric and cumin in the marinade are an added plus.

Sprightly Spiced Roast Chicken

SERVES 4

1 free-range/organic chicken,
  weighing about 1.5kg/3lb
1 glass of white wine to make
  the sauce/gravy
salt
1 tbsp olive oil

FOR THE MARINADE
juice of 1 large lemon
2 tbsp olive oil
2 garlic cloves, peeled and crushed
1 tsp turmeric
2 tsp cumin powder

1 Mix the marinade ingredients together in a small bowl.

2 Put the chicken in a large bowl and pour/brush/smooth the marinade over. Turn the bird in the marinade and leave for a few hours, covered, in the fridge.

3 Preheat the oven to 180°C/350°F/Gas Mark 4. Bring the chicken to room temperature. Sprinkle some salt over the bird and place it, breast down, in a large roasting pan. Pour any marinade remaining in the bowl over the chicken. Add a further tablespoon of olive oil and place in the middle of the oven. Roast for 45 minutes, basting it from time to time with the juices.

4 Turn the bird over and roast for a further 30 minutes.

5 Let the chicken rest while you make a sauce from the juices. Tip the pan and spoon out all but a tablespoon of the fat. Add the white wine and stir, dissolving the bits of residue in the sauce on the hob over a low heat.

Served here with roasted sweet potatoes

A bowl of our cherry tomatoes waiting their turn reminded me of this delicious Marcella Hazan recipe – a different summer way with chicken. Their sweetness is balanced by the touch of bitterness offered by the little black olives from Nice.

Pan-roasted Chicken with Cherry Tomatoes

SERVES 4

1 free-range/organic chicken,
   weighing about 1.5kg/3lb, cut up into
   8–10 pieces
1 tbsp olive oil
2 tsp rosemary needles, finely chopped
5 garlic cloves, peeled and left whole
salt and pepper
100ml/3½ fl oz white wine
1 small dry red chilli, left whole
   (optional)
20+ cherry tomatoes
a handful of black olives

1 Trim any excess fat, tidying up some of the loose skin from the chicken.

2 Heat the olive oil in a large sauté pan with a lid. Add the rosemary and garlic. Put in the chicken pieces, skin side down, and sauté them over a medium-high heat. Nudge them with a spoon after 2–3 minutes; when they move easily without sticking to the pan, look to see if they've nicely browned. At that point, turn them over and repeat on the reverse side.

3 When you have a pan of golden chicken pieces, season them generously and add the wine and the chilli (if using). Let it bubble a little, then cover the pan and cook the chicken for about 30 minutes on a low heat, turning the pieces from time to time to keep them moist. Add a tablespoon or two of water if needed. Add the tomatoes and olives and cover the pan again.

4 Cook until the skins of the tomatoes show signs of splitting, about 10 minutes, taking care not to overcook the breasts.

This is more northern France than Mediterranean – the butter and cider point to Normandy rather than Provence for its provenance. It is a practical all-in-one-pot recipe to dish up with some brown basmati rice or quinoa. Adapted from Jenny Baker's handy *Kitchen Suppers*, it's a flavoursome way to cook guinea fowl – a gamier-tasting alternative to chicken.

Pot Roast Guinea Fowl with Cider, Fennel and Apples

SERVES 4

2 large apples (Cox's, Fuji), peeled, cored and quartered
1 fennel bulb, outer casing removed and cut into quarters, or eighths if large
½ tsp cinnamon powder
30g/1oz butter
1 tbsp olive oil
150ml/¼ pint dry cider
1 guinea fowl, cut into 6 pieces (2 wings, 2 legs, 2 breasts – larger pieces stay moist)
salt and pepper
2 tbsp yogurt, whisked smooth (optional but gives the sauce a little more depth)
cooked brown basmati rice or quinoa, to serve

1 In a casserole, fry the apple and fennel pieces, sprinkled with cinnamon, in half the butter and olive oil for 5–10 minutes. Set aside with the juices in a bowl.

2 Boil the cider in the same pan to reduce it to roughly 3 tablespoons and pour it over the apples.

3 Season the guinea fowl all over and brown it on a medium heat in the remaining butter and oil.

4 Return the apples, fennel and sauce to the casserole. Cover and cook on a low heat for 30 minutes. The juices should run clear when the thigh is pierced – if they are still pinkish, cook a little longer.

5 Transfer the guinea fowl pieces, the apples and fennel from the casserole to a warmed plate. Let the juices cool a little in the pan, then whisk in the yogurt to make a sauce. Carefully pour into a heated jug. Serve with brown basmati rice or quinoa.

This reminds me of meals round the kitchen table at home in the fifties. It's simple and inexpensive and would possibly stretch to a second meal – important factors for my mother, with a husband and three sons to feed on limited means. Nothing exotic – except a little kick from the chillis, olives and peppers (optional) – comfort food, really. The low temperature of the oven helps keep the chicken moist, but you need to test for doneness. If the juices run pink when you insert the tip of a knife into a leg joint, it needs a little more time.

Chicken Casserole

SERVES 4

3 tbsp olive oil
125g/4oz bacon/pancetta, diced small
3 sticks or a heart of celery, chopped small
1 onion, peeled and chopped small
1 garlic clove, peeled and chopped
salt and pepper
1 free range/organic chicken, weighing about 1.5kg/3lb, cut into 8–10 pieces, washed and dried
250g/8oz tinned drained tomatoes, chopped roughly into a mush
125ml/4 fl oz white wine
125ml/4 fl oz stock (I use organic vegetable stock cubes)
3 small fresh red chillis, kept whole
3–4 sprigs of rosemary
1 red pepper, deseeded and cut into thin strips (optional, but adds colour to the dish)
a handful of juicy black olives, pitted if you have the time
a handful of parsley, chopped
baked sweet potatoes or brown basmati rice, to serve

1 Preheat the oven to 160°C/325°C/Gas Mark 3.

2 Heat a tablespoon of olive oil in a large frying pan and sauté the bacon or pancetta, celery, onion and garlic gently for about 20 minutes, allowing them to colour and concentrating the taste. Spoon the mixture into an ovenproof casserole.

3 Season the chicken pieces and heat another spoonful of oil in the frying pan. Sauté them on a highish heat, turning as they brown. Add them to the casserole.

4 Add the tomatoes to the frying pan and stir vigorously. Add the wine and stock, scraping the residue into the mix. Carefully pour this into the casserole.

5 Tuck in the whole chillis and the rosemary sprigs. Turn over the contents, cover the casserole and bring to a simmer on the stovetop.

6 Transfer the covered casserole to the oven and cook for a further 30 minutes.

7 While in the oven, heat the remaining olive oil in the pan and gently sauté the strips of pepper (if using).

8 Add the peppers and olives to the casserole after 30 minutes and cook, uncovered, for a further 15 minutes in the oven. (This can be done on the stovetop too.)

9 Sprinkle with chopped parsley and serve. We serve with baked sweet potato, but it would also be delicious with basmati rice.

Nothing exotic –
except a little kick
from the chillis,
olives and peppers –
comfort food, really.

Meat

Meat – in this case, beef, pork and lamb – does not play a leading role in our day-to-day eating scenario. We eat it, and enjoy it, occasionally. How times have changed. I remember 'meat and two veg' being the mantra of what we aspired to eat every day in the 1950s, as my father aspired to earn £1,000 a year! I suppose the emphasis in those days on getting enough meat to grow up 'healthy, wealthy and wise' was a reaction to the long years of rationing when people ate no meat or very little. Now we must limit our intake of red meat, it is said, and make sure we eat our five portions of vegetables and fruit a day. Sounds good to me. But a slice or two of pork fillet with a spoonful of balsamic onion sauce (page 146), or a helping of the Slow-roast Leg of Lamb (page 152) with Mint Sauce with Apple and Onion (page 69) sounds good too – from time to time.

This lovely autumn/winter comfort dish is based on one by the talented Frances Bissell.

Pork Chops and White Beans Baked in Orange Juice

SERVES 4

2 x 400g/13oz tins or bottles white
   beans, drained and rinsed
4 spare rib chops (*côtes d'échines* in
   France – these are the tastier ones)
1 onion, peeled and sliced
1 stick celery, sliced
2 oranges
1 tsp coriander seeds
150ml/5 fl oz stock
salt and pepper
chopped fresh coriander (cilantro)
   or parsley

1 Preheat the oven to 160°C/325°F/Gas Mark 3. Put the beans in the oven dish you will serve from.

2 Dry-fry the chops to brown well in a non-stick pan. Lay on top of the beans.

3 Brown the onion and celery in the same pan – the fat from the chops will be enough to fry them in. Spread over the chops.

4 Carefully trim some strips of zest from one of the oranges. Bury these in with the chops and beans. Squeeze the juice from both oranges over the chops.

5 Crush the coriander seeds in a pestle and mortar and sprinkle over. Add the stock.

6 Bake in the oven for 2 hours. Check after an hour that there is enough liquid, but be careful not to add too much stock or the concentrated taste of the sauce will weaken. Season when cooked and sprinkle over the coriander or parsley to serve.

This is a very versatile dish adapted from one in the first River Cafe cookbook. It is good for company – you could cook two 1.5kg/3lb pieces of loin side by side; it would take no longer and you will have enough for at least twelve. It goes very well with the White Bean Gratin (page 175), which you can cook in the oven while the pork is resting, covered in foil, for half an hour.

Pork Loin Roasted in Balsamic Vinegar

SERVES 4
salt and pepper
1kg/2lb pork fillet, rind and most
  of the fat removed
50g/2oz butter
2 tbsp olive oil
2–3 good-size red onions, peeled and
  cut into thickish slices, top to bottom
1 good tbsp rosemary, chopped
350ml/12 fl oz balsamic vinegar
60ml/2 fl oz red wine

1 Preheat the oven to 220°C/425°F/Gas Mark 7.

2 Season the meat well. Brown it thoroughly on all sides, on a cast-iron grill if possible. Set it aside.

3 Put a roasting pan on a medium to low heat on the hob.

4 Add the butter and olive oil, and gently soften the sliced onions for 5 minutes (not too long or they'll burn up too easily when in the oven).

5 Stir in the rosemary. Add the pork and half the balsamic vinegar. Turn the pork until it is well coated.

6 Put the pan in the oven and roast the pork for 35–40 minutes depending on the thickness of the fillet. It's best to check it at 35 minutes as you want to keep it moist but not too pink. After the first 10 minutes, turn the pork and onions briefly in the sauce.

7 Five minutes before taking the pork out, add the remaining balsamic vinegar. The onion may look rather burnt – adding the balsamic moistens it again.

8 Then out with the pork and let it rest, covered with foil. Deglaze the pan with the wine and balance the taste – you may need a little more wine.

9 To serve, slice the pork really thin and add some sauce to each plate, with extra in a sauceboat on the table. I usually put three pieces of pork on each plate.

. . . a very versatile dish . . . It is good for company – you could cook two 1.5kg/3lb pieces of loin side by side and you will have enough for at least twelve.

It's all in the name! This is the tenderest part of a pork loin. A pound and a half (750g) will feed four easily, maybe six, and as tenderloins are usually of similar dimensions, this allows you to double up easily. A good dish for company, it's also delicious cold.

Roasted Pork Tenderloin

SERVES 4
1 tenderloin of pork – most of the fat
  trimmed away
1 tbsp olive oil

FOR THE MARINADE
1 garlic clove, peeled and pulped
  with 1 tsp salt
1 tsp Dijon mustard
spears of a branch of rosemary, chopped
leaves of several thyme branches
salt and pepper
3 tbsp olive oil

1 Whisk the marinade ingredients together in a large bowl. Bathe the tenderloin in it, then put the meat in a plastic box or bag and leave in the fridge overnight. Let it come back to room temperature before taking it out of the box/bag.

2 Preheat the oven to 200°C/400°F/Gas Mark 6.

3 To seal the meat, heat 1 tablespoonful of olive oil in an ovenproof pan. When hot, seal the tenderloin, turning as it browns. Put the pan in the oven and cook for about 20 minutes.

4 After 15 minutes, check it for doneness by gently pressing down on the meat with a finger or thumb. It should be supple but not too supple. You can slice into the centre of the loin to check, too. Ideally the meat will have a faintly pinkish tinge, though if the juices run pink, cook for a couple of minutes more. Try not to overcook as this will render the meat leathery. You can use a meat thermometer, of course. The US Department of Agriculture recently lowered the temperature considered safe for pork to 62°C/144°F.

Based on a wonderful recipe by Australian chef Skye Gyngell. Serve with the courgettes (zucchini) (on page 81) mixed into the meat.

Slow-cooked Shoulder of Lamb

SERVES 4–5
1 shoulder of lamb
sea salt and black pepper
2 fresh bay leaves
1 bunch sage
1 dried red chilli, crumbled
2 anchovies
5 garlic cloves, left whole and unpeeled
2 large glasses white wine
2 tbsp red wine vinegar
Courgettes (zucchini) with Garlic and Parsley (page 81), to serve
chopped parsley, to serve

1 Preheat the oven to 160°C/325°F/Gas Mark 3.

2 Carefully trim the lamb shoulder of most of its fat. Season well with salt and pepper.

3 Brown in a large pan over medium-high heat. The shoulder is not the ideal shape for this manoeuvre – do the best you can.

4 Transfer it to a large baking tray. Add the bay leaves, sage, chilli, anchovies and whole garlic cloves. Pour over the white wine and vinegar. Cover the tray with foil – it's important to do this carefully – otherwise you may find that the liquid dries up during the long cooking time. Place on the middle shelf of the oven.

5 Cook for 2½ hours, checking after 1½ hours to see if the liquid needs topping up.

6 Remove the foil and cook for a further 30 minutes to brown the meat a little more. Ten minutes before the lamb is ready, cook the courgettes (zucchini), as per page 81.

7 Remove the lamb from the oven (it should be soft enough to eat with a spoon). Pull the meat from the bone, discarding the shoulder blade, and arrange on a serving platter. Add the courgettes (zucchini). Sprinkle over some parsley and serve.

This superb dish for company is adapted from one in Frances Bissell's exceptional book, *The Pleasures of Cookery*.

Lamb Tagine

SERVES 8

2kg/4lb boned shoulder of lamb, as much fat as possible trimmed away, ending up with about 1.5kg/3lb lean lamb, cut into 2.5cm/1in cubes
3 tbsp olive oil
3 onions, peeled and sliced
4 garlic cloves, peeled and chopped
1½ tsp cumin seeds
1½ tsp coriander seeds
900ml/1½ pints stock
24 dried apricots, halved
salt and pepper
a handful of parsley, or even better, coriander (cilantro), chopped
2 large tins flageolet beans, drained and rinsed (approx 500g)
steamed bulgur wheat, to serve

1 Preheat the oven to 160°C/325°F/Gas Mark 3.

2 Seal the meat in hot oil, using a large frying pan. When nicely browned, transfer to the ovenproof casserole you will serve it from.

3 Gently fry the onions and garlic in the fat and oil left in the pan, without browning them.

4 Fold in the whole spices and let them cook a little.

5 Add almost all the stock, leaving just enough in which to heat up the beans, and heat until reduced a little.

6 Add the apricots. Season this mixture and pour it into the casserole. Add a handful of parsley or coriander.

7 Heat the beans in a little stock in a separate pan and when hot add to the casserole.

8 Turn everything over carefully. Bring to a simmer on the hob and then place the tagine on a low shelf in the oven. Cook for 2 hours, checking after an hour to see if it needs topping up with stock – being careful not to lose the intensity of the sauce.

9 Serve over bulgur wheat.

The White Bean Gratin (page 175) and Mint Sauce with Apple and Onion (page 69) go well with this dish, adapted from the *River Cafe Cook Book*, as would some roast tomatoes.

Slow-roast Leg of Lamb

SERVES 6–8

3kg/6½lb leg of lamb
garlic slivers to lard the leg
olive oil
salt and pepper
200–250ml/7–9 fl oz milk

1 Preheat the oven to 200°C/400°F/Gas Mark 6.

2 In a roasting tray make slits in the fatty side of the lamb. Insert the garlic slivers – I don't think you can have too many; the tedium of doing it sets in after a while, though! Rub the lamb all over with olive oil, salt and pepper.

3 Put the lamb in its roasting tray into the oven and roast for 15 minutes. Then lower the heat to 150°C/300°F/Gas Mark 2 and cook for 3 hours.

4 Take the lamb out of the tray, place on a warm plate and cover with foil. Skim the fat off the juices. Place the pan over a medium heat on top of the stove. When it is very hot, add the milk. Stir and scrape all the good bits stuck to the pan into the sauce. Lower the heat and cook it gently until the sauce is a lovely nutty brown.

'Simply' bathe, season and grill! The timing for cooking does depend on the thickness of the chops, of course. Serve with a simple tomato and onion salad in summer or in winter, the Melting Tomatoes recipe (page 36) goes particularly well.

Simply Grilled Lamb Chops

SERVES 2

4 tbsp olive oil

bay leaves/rosemary/thyme, any one or all

a couple of garlic cloves, peeled and finely sliced

2 lemons

4 lamb chops

salt and pepper

1 Mix together the olive oil, herbs, garlic and the juice of one of the lemons. Add the chops and leave them to bathe in the mixture for a couple of hours.

2 Heat the grill to hot.

3 Place the chops on a grill pan and leave under the heat for 3 minutes without moving. Turn over and season the uncooked side. Grill for a further 3 minutes or so. For a pinkish finish, the chops should spring back after you press them gently with your index finger.

4 Quarter the second lemon and offer the pieces for squeezing over the succulent chops.

Another handy winter dish originating from Marcella Hazan. It's a meal in one; you don't need anything else apart from plenty of the mustard of your choice, although you could follow it with a crisp green salad.

Sausages Cooked with Red Cabbage

SERVES 4
10 tbsp olive oil
2 garlic cloves, peeled and chopped
1kg/2lb red cabbage, quartered,
   stemmed and finely sliced
1kg/2lb good pork sausages
salt and pepper

1 Put the olive oil and garlic in a large sauté pan or casserole (something that will hold the initially bulky pile of cabbage) and fry gently until nicely golden.

2 Add the cabbage and turn it well in the oil and garlic. Let it reduce gently, turning it from time to time while the cabbage cooks.

3 Put the sausages in a frying pan. Brown them all over.

4 When the cabbage has reduced (this can take about 30 minutes of gentle cooking), add salt and pepper and the sausages. Cook them together, the sausages buried in the cabbage, for another 20 minutes, turning them over from time to time.

A meal in one; you
don't need anything
else apart from
plenty of the mustard
of your choice . . .

Pasta

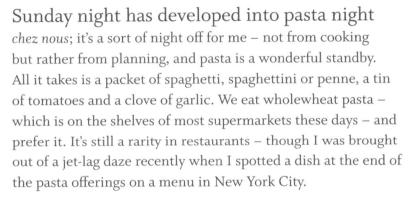

Sunday night has developed into pasta night *chez nous*; it's a sort of night off for me – not from cooking but rather from planning, and pasta is a wonderful standby. All it takes is a packet of spaghetti, spaghettini or penne, a tin of tomatoes and a clove of garlic. We eat wholewheat pasta – which is on the shelves of most supermarkets these days – and prefer it. It's still a rarity in restaurants – though I was brought out of a jet-lag daze recently when I spotted a dish at the end of the pasta offerings on a menu in New York City.

How *al dente* it's cooked is a matter of taste. In Italy you'd think it was an arrestable offence to overcook pasta – they cook it *al very dente* and it makes for agreeably slower eating. I tend to stick with 'the ones we love!' but here you'll find a few more of the endless possibilities . . .

This is a great pasta – a little different. It takes a bit of organising of ingredients beforehand, but is well worth it.

Broccoli Pasta

SERVES 2–3

salt
500g/1lb broccoli, cut into small florets
200g/7oz short dry wholewheat pasta, such as farfalle or penne
5 tbsp olive oil
2 garlic cloves, peeled and thinly sliced
8 anchovy fillets, mashed
3 small chilli peppers, cored and finely finely chopped with their seeds
50g/2oz freshly grated Parmesan cheese
1 tbsp dry-roasted pine nuts, if you have them
50g/2oz toasted breadcrumbs, wholewheat or rye

1 Bring a large saucepan full of water to the boil – salt well. Cook the broccoli in the water until it's just tender. Lift it out and into a warm bowl.

2 Bring the broccoli-scented water back to the boil, slip in the pasta and stir it once to stop it sticking to the bottom.

3 Meanwhile, heat the olive oil in a small pan and add the garlic. Cook it on a low heat to avoid it burning. When it begins to colour, take the pan off the heat and add the anchovies, stirring to make a sauce – add a tablespoon of the hot water to help it meld.

4 Add the chillies and put the pan back on a very low heat.

5 When the pasta is ready to your taste, drain it and return to the hot saucepan. Add the broccoli, the sauce and the cheese to it. Turn everything over, carefully coating the broccoli and the pasta in the oily sauce.

6 Heat a serving bowl and fold the mixture into it.

7 Sprinkle the pine nuts (if using) and the breadcrumbs on top – to be mixed in after you have presented the dish triumphantly to your guests!

This is adapted from a recipe in Marcella Hazan's *Marcella's Kitchen* and is a year-round wonder. It is quick and easy to make and has a distinctive earthy flavour, thanks to the rosemary. It's worth taking care to slice the garlic very thinly.

Penne with Rosemary and Balsamic Vinegar

SERVES 4

4 garlic cloves, peeled and very thinly sliced
8 tbsp olive oil
2 sprigs rosemary or 2½ tsp dried rosemary
600g/20oz tinned tomatoes, i.e. 2 large tins, drained of juice
salt and pepper
400g/13oz penne or farfalle or a mix of the two
2 tsp balsamic vinegar
freshly grated Parmesan, to serve

1. Sauté the garlic gently in the olive oil with the rosemary (if using fresh) until the garlic sizzles.

2. Add the tomatoes, 1–2 teaspoons salt and plenty of pepper. If using dried rosemary, add it with the tomatoes. Cook for 10–15 minutes.

3. Meanwhile, cook the pasta in well-salted boiling water.

4. Drain the pasta and add to the sauce. Cook for a minute or two – turning the pasta in the sauce. Turn off the heat, make a well in the middle of the pasta and add the balsamic vinegar. Again, turn the pasta thoroughly in the sauce.

5 Serve with freshly grated Parmesan cheese.

Based on Anna Del Conte's simple and delicious recipe, in which the tinned tuna is uncooked. It's good to use lovely ripe tomatoes in summer, but tinned tomatoes are better the rest of the year. These quantities might stretch to four as a starter, in which case add another 100g/4oz of pasta.

Spaghettini with Tuna and Tomato Sauce

SERVES 2

1–2 garlic cloves (I like 2), peeled and sliced

6 tbsp olive oil

500g/1lb ripe tomatoes, peeled and chopped or 1 x 400g/13oz tin tomatoes, drained and chopped

10 black Greek olives, pitted and cut into strips

1 tbsp capers, drained and squeezed

salt and pepper

12 fresh basil leaves or a good tablespoon of chopped parsley

200g/7oz spaghettini

1 x 200g/7oz tin good tuna

1 Put the garlic in a small pan with half the olive oil, the tomatoes, olives and the capers.

2 Bring to the boil and add some salt and the basil or parsley. Cook at a gentle simmer for 10 minutes or so. Meanwhile, boil a large pan of water, salt it and add the pasta.

3 Drain the tuna into a serving bowl, and add the remaining oil and plenty of pepper.

4 When the pasta is done, drain it, reserving a little of the liquid to loosen the sauce if necessary, and add it to the tuna.

5 Pour over the tomato sauce and mix it well.

This is a comforting pasta for the winter months. Most of the ingredients are store cupboard-based staples.

Tuna Pasta

SERVES 4

6 tbsp olive oil, plus extra to serve
2 garlic cloves, peeled and chopped
3 tbsp parsley, chopped
400g/13oz tin tomatoes, chopped
salt and pepper
400g/13oz wholewheat spaghettini
   or spaghetti
400g/13oz tinned tuna (drained
   weight), broken up
50g/2oz butter

1 . Heat the olive oil in a small pan and add the garlic.

2 When it begins to colour, add the parsley and stir for 30 seconds. Add the chopped tomatoes.

3 Cook for about 25 minutes, until the sauce gains an unctuous quality.

4 Meanwhile, bring a large pan of water to the boil and salt it. Add the pasta and cook it until it's done to your taste. Some like it more *al dente* than others; you have to keep testing it.

5 While the pasta is cooking, and when the sauce is ready, add the tuna to the sauce and mix it in thoroughly. When it's hot, add the butter and let it melt in. Season well – lots of pepper.

6 Drain the pasta, put it in a warmed bowl and add the sauce. Mix the two thoroughly and serve on warmed plates with a little extra olive oil drizzled over.

This is Frances Bissell's take on a lovely pasta dish. The taste is more authentic if you shell the walnuts yourself, but you need a little time. You could give the task to a guest who says, as guests sometimes do: 'Is there anything I can do?'!

Spaghettini with Walnut, Garlic and Parmesan Sauce

SERVES 4

100g/4oz shelled walnuts – be careful, if you shell them yourself, to avoid any teeth-cracking bits being left in

2 garlic cloves, peeled and crushed

1 tbsp parsley, chopped, plus a little extra parsley

salt and pepper

5 tbsp olive oil, plus extra to serve

1 tbsp walnut oil

425g/14oz wholewheat spaghettini or spaghetti

100g/4oz freshly grated Parmesan cheese, plus extra to serve

1 Put the walnuts, garlic and parsley in a food processor, season with salt and pepper, add the oils and pulse to a smooth sauce. Check the seasoning and adjust if necessary.

2 Cook the pasta in plenty of boiling salted water. Drain it, keeping a little of the cooking liquid, and put it back in the hot pan. Add the sauce, the cheese and a tablespoon of the cooking liquid and turn it over thoroughly.

3 Turn it into a warmed bowl of choice and sprinkle with the extra parsley. Serve immediately with more olive oil and Parmesan to hand.

The taste is more authentic if you shell the walnuts yourself, but you need a little time.

This sauce is like a pesto. You can prepare the nut mix beforehand and reheat it very gently when you come to cook the pasta – stress-free cooking, in principle! Hazelnuts roasted are particularly moreish. Mixed with olive oil, chillies and garlic, and served, as here, with nutty wholewheat pasta, they are irresistible!

Hazelnut Pasta

SERVES 2

3 tbsp olive oil

1 tsp hazelnut oil, if available

2 garlic cloves, peeled and pulped in a mortar

2 small dry chillies, chopped

75g/3oz roasted hazelnuts (see method), chopped (I use the small container of a food processor and pulse the nuts to control the finished size – crunchy little bits, not powder)

2–3 tbsp parsley, chopped

salt

200g/7oz wholewheat penne or spaghettini

50g/2oz Parmesan cheese, grated, plus extra to serve, if liked

2 tbsp pecorino cheese, if available (bear in mind its saltiness)

1 Heat both the oils in a pan and add the garlic. Colour it gently, taking care not to let it burn. Turn off the heat and remove the garlic from the pan to prevent it burning – a sieve with a metal net does this safely – and set it aside to cool.

2 Add the chillies to the warm oil in the pan. Gently reheat the oil and chillies in the pan. Add the hazelnuts and the parsley and cook briefly over a low heat – about 3 minutes. Turn off the heat and mix in the sautéed garlic.

3 Bring a large saucepan of water to the boil with a dash of salt. Add the pasta and cook it to taste. When the pasta is done as you like it, drain, reserving 2–3 tablespoons of the water.

4 Return the pasta to the warm pan you cooked it in and add the nuts and parsley mixture and the cheese(s) and mix thoroughly. Add the reserved pasta water to loosen the sauce a little. Add salt to taste. Serve immediately (it cools down quickly), with extra cheese and a swirl of olive oil if you like.

TO ROAST THE HAZELNUTS

Preheat the oven to 180°C/350°F/Gas Mark 4. Spread the hazelnuts over a shallow oven tray and put in the oven. Check them after 5 minutes – it depends on their size how long they take. Taste one to check for crunchy doneness; roast them a little longer if you feel they need it. Let the nuts cool before processing them.

Farmhouse cupboard fare: olive oil, garlic, tomatoes, chillies, pasta and Parmesan – it's that simple! A classic example of the Mediterranean way of eating, which is in the news, again. In fact, it has barely been out of the news. Stories of people living to very advanced ages on Greek islands crop up with annoying regularity on the health pages; annoying in the sense that you immediately want to go there and get a slice of the action!

Penne Arrabiata

4 tbsp olive oil

3 large garlic cloves, peeled and pulped in a mortar

4 small dried red chillies, chopped with their seeds (less or more depending on your tolerance and taste, but this is called 'angry' [*arrabiata*] penne!)

2 x 400g/13oz tins tomatoes, chopped and with their liquid

salt

400g/13oz wholewheat penne rigate (the ridged kind, which picks up the sauce better)

Grated Parmesan to serve, if liked

1 Gently heat the oil in a pan large enough to take the pasta too. Slip in the pulped garlic and let it colour lightly. Add the chillies and the chopped tomatoes. Cook until the sauce thickens – about 30 minutes – stirring regularly. It should be a thick pool of red glory.

2 Bring a large saucepan of water to the boil and add a teaspoon of salt. Add the penne, stir to stop the pasta sticking to the base of the pan and bring back to the boil. Cook until just tender.

3 Drain well and add the penne to the sauce. Turn to coat the pasta thoroughly. Serve with grated Parmesan if that suits, and a glass of hearty red wine.

This is a delicious sauce, and so simple – made in 5 minutes while the pasta is cooking. Our friend Hilton McRae made it for us in London. My version is a slight twist on his, using olive oil instead of butter and adding lemon zest.

Spaghettini with Garlic, Lemon Zest and Rosemary

SERVES 2

200g/7oz wholewheat spaghettini
  or spaghetti
4 tbsp olive oil
3 sprigs of fresh rosemary
3 garlic cloves, peeled and pulped in
  a mortar
1 vegetable stock cube, crumbled
2 tbsp Parmesan, grated
zest of 1 lemon
some chopped parsley

1 Cook the pasta in salted water until al dente or to your taste.

2 Meanwhile, heat the olive oil in a small saucepan and on a low heat cook the rosemary sprigs and garlic until the garlic begins to colour – about 5 minutes.

3 Add the crumbled stock cube, stir thoroughly and turn off the heat.

4 Drain the pasta and put it in a warm bowl. Strain the oil through a sieve and add it to the pasta with the cheese. Turn it over to coat the pasta with the oil and sprinkle the lemon zest and parsley on top. You could pick the not-too-brown garlic bits out of the sieve and scatter them over the pasta too!

Gratin and All-in-one Dishes

Gratins and all-in-one dishes come to the table with 'eat me' written all over them – often sizzlingly so. There's work involved in assembling them for the oven and the pre-cooking of an ingredient (the aubergines [eggplant] in the Melanzane Parmigiana on page 176, the frying of chickpeas [garbanzo beans] in the gratin with chorizo and spinach on page 180 etc.), but this process can be enjoyable. When done hours in advance, it also makes these dishes a less stressful choice for when company arrives. Pop them in the oven and keep an eye out while you chat to your guests. They will be impressed.

A meal-in-a-pot dish, inspired by a Nigel Slater recipe in a newspaper clipping I found recently.

Sweet Potato, Fennel and Smoky Bacon au Gratin

SERVES 2–3

2 tbsp olive oil

1 onion, peeled and chopped

2 sticks of celery, chopped

3 garlic cloves, peeled and pulped with a tsp of salt

1 tsp rosemary leaves, finely chopped

50g/2oz smoked bacon, cubed

1 tsp smoked paprika

250g/8oz cooked chickpeas (garbanzo beans) (see page 217 if using dried)

1 medium sweet potato, peeled and sliced into thickish rounds, these halved and halved again if necessary

1 fennel bulb, outer leaves removed, sliced thickish on the vertical and similarly halved

300ml/½ pint stock

200ml/7 fl oz coconut cream

salt and pepper

2 tbsp grated Parmesan cheese mixed with 2 tbsp breadcrumbs

1 Preheat the oven to 190°C/375°F/Gas Mark 5. Heat the olive oil in a medium-sized shallow sauté pan. Fry the onion and celery for a couple of minutes over a medium heat.

2 Add the garlic, rosemary, bacon and paprika. Stir these together and continue cooking, stirring as the vegetables begin to soften and the bacon colours, for about 10 minutes.

3 Turn the chickpeas into the pan and stir them in. Add the sweet potato and the fennel, and mix them in. Slowly add the stock and the coconut cream, stirring. Season with salt and pepper. Bring it to the boil and sprinkle over the Parmesan and breadcrumb mixture.

4 Place in the middle of the oven and bake for about 30 minutes.

5 Meredith likes to sprinkle a little chopped parsley over the finished dish, for the look.

At the time of writing it's Oscars time of year, so categories are on my mind. Celery often features *chez nous*; sometimes in bit parts – literally – as one element of a *soffritto*, the finely chopped mixture of vegetables known as *mirepoix* in French, or in a supporting role as a dipping stick for sauces like anchoïade, hummus or guacamole. Here, it comes out of the shadows and into the spotlight to take the lead, with a strong supporting cast. It can be assembled beforehand – overnight, in fact – and popped in the oven shortly before you are ready to eat.

Celery au Gratin

SERVES 2 AS A MAIN COURSE,
4 AS A SIDE DISH

750g/1½lb celery (weigh after separating the sticks and discarding the damaged outer ones), cut into short pieces
30g/1oz smoked bacon, as much fat as possible removed, and chopped small
1 onion, peeled and chopped
2 garlic cloves, peeled and chopped
1 tbsp olive oil
3 large tins tomatoes, chopped
1 level tsp cayenne pepper
sprigs of thyme and a couple of bay leaves
salt and pepper
2 tbsp dry white wine
12 juicy black olives, pitted and halved
3 tbsp Parmesan cheese, grated

1 Steam the celery until tender and set aside. (Alternatively, simmer in 600ml/1 pint of stock.)

2 Preheat the oven to 220°C/425°F/Gas Mark 7.

3 Sauté the bacon, onion and garlic in the olive oil in a large sauté pan until they start to colour.

4 Add the chopped tomatoes with the cayenne pepper, herbs and a pinch of salt. Cook these gently for 5 minutes.

5 Add the wine and cook for another couple of minutes to let the wine evaporate.

6 Add the olives and cook for a couple of minutes.

7 Turn off the heat and add the celery, turning it over thoroughly in the sauce.

8 Spread a layer of the celery mix over the base of an ovenproof gratin dish. Season and sprinkle over some Parmesan. Repeat the process – seasoning and sprinkling cheese over each layer. Finish with a layer of Parmesan. Place the dish on the highest shelf in the oven and bake for 20–30 minutes, checking after 20 minutes. The gratin should come out sizzling with a pleasingly charred look. Let it rest for 15 minutes before serving.

This is a good accompaniment to Slow-roast Leg of Lamb (page 152) or the Roasted Pork Tenderloin (page 148). It would serve vegetarians as a main course at the same meal.

White Bean Gratin

SERVES 6

1kg/2lb prepared (i.e. either from dry, tinned or preferably, bottled) white beans
3 generous tbsp crème fraîche
salt and pepper
2 generous tbsp grated Parmesan
2 generous tbsp dry wholewheat breadcrumbs
30g/1oz butter, melted

1 Preheat the oven to 200°C/400°F/Gas Mark 6.

2 Drain and rinse the beans and put them in a bowl.

3 Add the crème fraîche, salt and pepper to taste. Don't stint on the former: you need enough cream to avoid them drying out in the oven but not so much they are overwhelmed. Mix carefully and thoroughly. Check the seasoning – a delicious exercise! – the pepper especially.

4 Arrange the beans evenly in a baking dish (preferably one that presents well at the table).

5 Mix the Parmesan and breadcrumbs well together, adding some salt and pepper.

6 Pour the melted butter over the breadcrumbs and Parmesan, and mix thoroughly. Cover the beans with the crumb mixture.

7 When you are ready, bake the gratin in the oven for about 20–30 minutes. It should be nicely browned on top and sizzling.

Parmigiana is Sicilian for the slats of a shutter and being a dish of layers, perhaps this is the origin of its name. Others say that the name derives simply from the name of the cheese used: Parmigiano Reggiano. Serve as a starter (cut the aubergines into rounds and follow the same steps below but build individual round pyramids on a small bed of mixed leaves, dressed as you like) or a light lunch or supper. Or you could serve it with roast chicken or meat.

Melanzane Parmigiana (Aubergine/Eggplant in Tomato Sauce with Parmesan)

SERVES 4
salt and pepper
2 medium aubergines (eggplant), sliced carefully lengthways, roughly 5mm/¼in thick – watch out for fingers!
Quick Tomato Sauce (page 70)
olive oil
Parmesan cheese

1 Salt the aubergine slices and leave in a colander over a bowl for a couple of hours to draw out the liquid. Put slices between sheets of kitchen paper to dry them thoroughly. Meanwhile, make the tomato sauce.

2 Preheat the oven to 200°C/400°F/Gas Mark 6.

3 Heat the grill to very hot. Brush the aubergine slices lightly with olive oil on one side. Place on the grill oiled side down. Brush the exposed side with oil. Check that the slices are cooking and after 3–4 minutes turn them over and cook for a further 3–4 minutes. A pair of tongs is useful here. Turn them back again if you like – both sides should be nicely charred and soft; undercooked aubergine is inedible. For an alternative method, see the recipe for Aubergine Slices with Walnut and Garlic Spread on page 34.

4 Lightly oil the bottom of your chosen baking dish, then cover with a layer of tomato sauce, followed by a layer of aubergines and topped by a sprinkling of Parmesan. Salt and pepper lightly at each stage. Repeat this process until you've used all the ingredients. Sprinkle the last layer of aubergines with a good covering of Parmesan.

5 Put the dish in the top of the oven and bake for about 20 minutes – checking a couple of times to make sure it's not burning. Then let it rest for a bit – it's best served tepid.

6 A delicious variation is the addition of 200g/7oz of sliced courgettes (zucchini) – treated and cooked as the aubergines – to the composition, to make it Melanzane e Zucchini Parmigiana!

This is a traditional dish that shows up all over Italy, though it signals 'the south' to me.

This traditional summer dish is adapted from two fabulous sources – Elizabeth David and Anna Del Conte. For lunch or supper, you just need a crisp green salad to accompany it.

Courgette (Zucchini) and Tomato Tian/Tortino

SERVES 4

3 or 4 medium courgettes (zucchini), sliced very thinly
salt and pepper
2 tbsp olive oil
2 onions, peeled and chopped
2 garlic cloves, peeled and thinly sliced
2 tbsp chopped parsley
250g/8oz tomatoes, fresh if good enough, otherwise tinned, drained and chopped
1 tsp dried oregano
3 tbsp grated Parmesan cheese
3 tbsp breadcrumbs, wholewheat or 100 per cent rye
extra olive oil

1 Lightly salt the courgettes and leave them to drain in a colander for an hour, then dry them thoroughly with kitchen paper or a clean tea towel (it's best to prepare them in advance).

2 Heat the olive oil in a large pan and fry the onions gently until they are pale golden and tinged with brown – about 15 minutes.

3 Stir in the garlic and parsley and let them cook gently for a couple of minutes.

4 Fold in the tomatoes and mix well. Let them cook together on a low heat for a good 10 minutes. (Elizabeth David makes the case for cooking the tomatoes beforehand – thus concentrating their taste – and mixing them into the courgettes just before the baking stage.)

5 Add the courgettes and turn them into the mixture. Cook, covered, for 15 minutes – until the courgettes begin to soften and become opaque.

6 Preheat the oven to 200°C/400°F/Gas Mark 6.

7 Uncover the pan and continue cooking for another 10 minutes. It's important that the mixture is not watery.

8 Season with salt, pepper and the oregano. Mix in the seasoning well and taste.

9 Brush a suitably sized and presentable shallow oven dish with oil and turn the mix into it.

10 Mix together the cheese and breadcrumbs and sprinkle these over the tian. Drizzle some olive oil in a filigree pattern over the top and bake for about 15–20 minutes – it should come out nicely browned and sizzling.

Adapted from a recipe by Mark Bittman of *The New York Times*, this is a great one-pan dish. This version should be enough for a light lunch for four, though the first time I made it Meredith and I polished off the whole lot! It could also serve as a delicious starter served over salad.

Gratin of Fried Chickpeas (Garbanzo Beans) with Chorizo and Spinach

SERVES 4

4 tbsp olive oil

500g/1lb bottled or tinned chickpeas (garbanzo beans), rinsed, drained and dried thoroughly

salt and pepper

100g/4oz spicy chorizo sausage, sliced and diced

250g/8oz spinach, washed and shaken dry

4 tbsp sherry

2–3 handfuls of wholewheat/rye breadcrumbs

extra olive oil

green salad, to serve

1 Heat 3 tablespoons of olive oil in a pan large enough to hold the chickpeas in one layer.

2 When hot, put in the chickpeas, season and turn down the heat a little. The object is to slowly crisp them up – allow about 10 minutes for this – shaking the pan from time to time and being careful not to let them burn.

3 When they have coloured nicely, add the chorizo and cook on in the same way for about 8 minutes. Empty the mix into a bowl.

4 Return the pan to the heat, add the remaining tablespoon of olive oil, the spinach, some seasoning and sprinkle the sherry over. Turn the spinach over and over as it melts, until the liquid has evaporated. Return the chickpea/chorizo mix to the pan and fold in the spinach.

5 Transfer this mix to a small gratin dish, sprinkle over the breadcrumbs and the extra olive oil. Put under a hot grill for about 3 minutes. Serve with a green salad.

This delectable one-pot dish gives you something to do with leftover Swiss chard stalks! A one-pot vegetarian dish or serve with pork chops or sausages – all done in the oven.

Gratin of Swiss Chard Stalks

SERVES 4

stalks from 1kg/2lb Swiss chard, cleaned up and cut into bite-size lengths
salt and pepper
2 tbsp Parmesan cheese, grated
olive oil

1 Preheat the oven to 200°C/400°F/Gas Mark 6.

2 Soften the stalks in plenty of salted boiling water for 5 minutes. Drain thoroughly.

3 In a small oiled gratin dish, arrange a layer of the stalks and sprinkle a tablespoon of Parmesan then a little olive oil over them and season lightly. Repeat this until all the stalks are in the dish. Sprinkle over the remaining cheese and a little more oil.

4 Cook in the uppermost part of the oven for 15–20 minutes.

5 Finish it off with a minute under a hot grill.

Grains and Pulses

I like lentils; the same goes for white beans and chickpeas (garbanzo beans) – all pulses, in fact. They have many uses and take on board countless flavourings. Some pulses, such as lentils and beans, have a reputation for causing flatulence. Well, it's true, there's no denying it, but for me their tastiness outweighs this minor inconvenience; but that's an individual choice. Meredith, for instance, takes some persuading. I also really like brown basmati rice and quinoa, but I can understand that for some they are a poor substitute for potatoes. In fact, they can offer rather more than the simple spud. I recently read this on the website *Passion for Pulses* under the title 'Pulses and Diabetes':

Pulses have a low glycemic index, making them excellent sources of carbohydrate in the diet of those affected by diabetes... Once referred to as 'poor man's meat' because they are high in protein and inexpensive, pulses are valuable additions to a modern diet [way of eating] because of their good taste, convenience, ease of use and nutritional role in managing and preventing diabetes.

Our friend, Tari Mandair (we call him the Carefree Cook, and he is an example to all us worryguts) is never panicked when people turn up unexpectedly and have to be fed. He looks to see how many extra guests are coming through the door and adds more water to the dal accordingly. If there is some left over, form it into little burger shapes, coat them with some chickpea (garbanzo bean) flour and fry in hot oil.

Comfort Lentils (otherwise known as Dal)

SERVES 4

500g/1lb red lentils
1 litre/1¾ pints vegetable stock
  (I use 1 vegetable stock cube per
  500ml/17 fl oz)
4 tbsp vegetable oil
1 medium onion, peeled and chopped
1 tsp coriander seeds, pounded in a
  pestle and mortar
1½ tsp cumin seeds, pounded in a
  pestle and mortar
1 tsp garam masala (page 215)
½ tsp chilli powder

1 Rinse the lentils very thoroughly – until the water shows clear.

2 Put them in a saucepan with the stock and bring gently to the boil. Turn the heat down to low and let them simmer, covered, stirring from time to time. They are done when a small puddle floats on the top. Turn them off.

3 Heat the vegetable oil in a small frying pan. Add the onion and fry until it is browning nicely.

4 Add the spices and mix them in well. Continue to cook gently to release the aroma.

5 Add the cooked spices and onion to the lentils and mix in thoroughly. Heat through and serve.

We often eat these
lentils with broccoli,
simply steamed, and
brown basmati rice.

Meredith tells me the first time she became aware of lentils was at the age of thirty-five. They had not been part of her experience growing up in suburban Chicago! Much has changed and Indian restaurants are now commonplace in the US. This recipe, adapted from a recipe in Ismail Merchant's excellent and quirky cookbook *Indian Cuisine*, is hands-on for the first half hour or so, as it builds in the taste. We ate it recently as an accompaniment to the Sprightly Spiced Roast Chicken (page 136).

Lemony Lentils

SERVES 4

1 small onion, peeled and chopped
2 tbsp olive oil
250g/8oz red lentils, rinsed until the water runs clear
1 short stick of cinnamon
1 tsp fresh ginger, grated
300ml/½ pint (approx) stock
300ml/½ pint (approx) hot water
1 tsp cayenne pepper
1 tsp salt
juice and the shell halves of 1 lemon

TO FINISH

2 tbsp olive oil
½ small onion, peeled and sliced
1 small dried red chilli, cored, deseeded and chopped
1 garlic clove, peeled and chopped

1 Cook the onion over a low heat in the olive oil until it is opaque – about 5 minutes.

2 Add the lentils, cinnamon and ginger, and mix in. Cook these together gently for about 10 minutes, keeping the heat low and stirring from time to time to avoid them sticking to the bottom of the pan and burning. A nutty aroma starts to rise from the darkening lentils as they cook.

3 Add the stock and hot water, the cayenne and salt, and bring to a simmer. Cook gently for a further 10 minutes, then add the lemon juice and the empty lemon halves and stir it all together. Cover the pan and continue cooking on a very low heat – use a heat diffuser if available – for 45 minutes, stirring occasionally to avoid sticking.

4 To finish, in a small frying pan heat the olive oil and add the sliced onion. Let this colour for 5 minutes over a medium heat. Add the chilli and chopped garlic and continue cooking until the garlic begins to brown. Add this to the lentils and mix it in.

You can serve this tepid as a salad or warmer as part of a meal, with salmon fillets, for example, leaving out the *labneh* (yogurt cheese) and walnuts. Goats' cheese is a good alternative to *labneh*.

Puy Lentils with Labneh and Dry Roasted Walnuts

SERVES 6

250g/8oz puy lentils, washed thoroughly
1 small onion, peeled and cut in half
2 garlic cloves, peeled
sprig of thyme and 2 bay leaves
1 tbsp red wine vinegar
4 tbsp olive oil
salt and pepper
1 large spring onion, peeled and chopped small (optional)
50g/2oz shelled walnuts, dry roasted
2 tbsp *labneh* (page 216) or goats' cheese

1 Put the lentils in a pan with enough water to cover them by 2.5cm/1in. Add the onion, garlic, thyme and bay leaves. Bring to the boil and simmer, covered, until the lentils are just done – about 25 minutes, depending on the packet instructions and the age of the lentils. If you leave them too long, they will be mushy (you may have to top up with more water).

2 Drain the lentils – ditching the herbs, the onion and garlic – and place them in a serving bowl.

3 Add the wine vinegar and the olive oil and turn them in carefully. Season with salt and pepper to taste.

4 Sprinkle the spring onion (if using), walnuts and *labneh* or goats' cheese on top.

These spicy little numbers made up a quick lunch recently, with grilled strips of marinated chicken breasts and Swiss chard leaves sautéed with garlic and olive oil. This is adapted from a lovely book of recipes by Australian cookery writer Jody Vassallo.

Spicy Chickpeas (Garbanzo Beans)

SERVES 4

2 tbsp olive oil

1 garlic clove, peeled and crushed to a paste with a little salt

1 tsp each smoked paprika, cumin powder, white pepper powder, coriander powder, cayenne powder, dried thyme and dried oregano

1 tsp salt

450g/16oz bottled or tinned chickpeas (garbanzo beans), rinsed, drained and dried thoroughly (it's important to dry them well; kitchen paper comes in handy here)

4 marinated chicken breasts, to serve

1 Put a tablespoon of the oil, the garlic, spices and dried herbs in a bowl and add the salt. Mix these thoroughly with a fork.

2 Add the chickpeas and turn them over to coat in the spice mixture.

3 Heat the remaining tablespoon of olive oil in a large frying pan. When the oil is hot, add the chickpeas and roll them about in the oil – they should ideally lie in one layer. Cook them over a gentle heat for 10 minutes, until they colour and crisp up.

4 The chickpeas are delicious served with a chicken breast each, cut into thin strips, seasoned and marinated in olive oil for an hour, then cooked on a hot grill for a couple of minutes each side.

This is delicious and a really useful accompanying vegetable that makes a good alternative to mashed potatoes.

Chickpea (Garbanzo Bean) Mash

SERVES 4

2 x 400g/13oz bottles/tins chickpeas, rinsed and drained
1 garlic clove, peeled and crushed
½ tsp chilli powder
salt and pepper
4 tbsp olive oil

1 Put the chickpeas, garlic, chilli powder, a teaspoon of salt and a few grinds of the peppermill in a food processor.

2 Add the oil and whizz. Add more oil if it's still too stiff.

3 Put the mix in a saucepan and gently heat it to hot. It will loosen up as it heats through. Adjust the seasoning.

These pancakes are street food, still sold on the streets of Nice and Marseille in southern France. They are about 20cm/8in in diameter and good for parking things on – a fried egg or some bacon bits or, as I did recently for a light supper, thinly sliced roast tomatoes, sprinkled with a little salt and olive oil and cooked for 20 minutes in a low oven (140°C/275°F/Gas Mark 1).

Farinata or Socca (Pancake)

SERVES 4

175g/6oz chickpea (garbanzo bean) flour
400ml/14 fl oz sparkling water
65ml/2.5 fl oz olive oil
salt and pepper
1 tbsp rosemary leaves
olive oil

1 Gently shake the flour through a sieve into a mixing bowl. Add the water and whisk it in until smooth.

2 Add the olive oil and whisk it in. Add pinches of salt and pepper and the rosemary. You will have roughly half a litre (20 fl oz) of batter. Leave to stand for 20–30 minutes.

3 When you are ready to make the pancake, heat a swirl of olive oil in a 25cm/10in frying pan. When hot, put a tablespoonful of the stirred mixture in the pan and turn the heat down a little. Cook for a few seconds until you can ease the pancake loose with a spatula or fish slice. Now you have to turn it over! Be bold! Practice makes perfect and anyway, the first attempt, if not completely successful, will be edible. Cook the pancake for another few seconds and remove from the pan. Both sides should be a golden brown. Add a few twists of the pepper mill to each side.

4 For a larger pancake, carefully pour a second tablespoon of batter on top of the first.

These white beans go well with sausages or a pork chop.

White Beans with Tomato, Sage and Garlic

SERVES 4
1 garlic clove, peeled and chopped
2 tbsp olive oil
½ tsp dried sage or a sprig of fresh sage
2 tinned tomatoes squashed in a little of
    their juice
½ vegetable stock cube dissolved in
    3 tbsp hot water
1 x 425g/14oz tin/jar white beans,
    drained and rinsed
salt and pepper

1 Lightly colour the garlic in the olive oil in a medium saucepan over a gentle heat.

2 Add the sage and stir a couple of times.

3 Add the tomatoes and let them cook gently for about 7 minutes.

4 Add the halved stock cube and the beans. Stir them in well, then cover and cook very gently for 10 minutes to let everything meld nicely. Add a little more hot water if things start to dry out.

5 Season with salt and plenty of pepper.

One of the oldest-known grains, quinoa is a useful alternative to rice. It takes less time to cook and is easily digestible. Sam Talbot is an American chef in his thirties. He has Type 1 diabetes and has written a delightful cookbook, illustrating the way he lives, eats and cooks, with a nicely ironic title, *The Sweet Life*. In his book he raves about quinoa; he eats it at least three times a week. This is his recipe, slightly adapted. The amount of liquid required is double the volume of the quinoa – easy to remember! Leaving the coriander and cumin seeds whole adds a nice crunchiness.

Sam's Quinoa

SERVES 4

2 tbsp olive oil
1 shallot, peeled and chopped small
1 tbsp coriander seeds
1 tsp cumin seeds
2 tbsp fresh ginger, chopped small
4 garlic cloves, peeled and pulped with
  some salt
175g/6oz red or white quinoa
480ml/16 fl oz stock
zest and juice of 1 lemon
a handful of chopped parsley

1 Heat the olive oil in a medium pan and sauté the shallot, spices and garlic for about 5 minutes to soften them.

2 Add the quinoa to the pan and turn it over with the spice mix. Add the stock, lemon zest and juice and bring it to a simmer. Cover the pan and turn the heat down to low. Cook for about 20 minutes.

3 Check to see how it's doing after 15 minutes and give it a stir. The grain should have absorbed all the liquid by the end of cooking. Sprinkle the parsley over and fork it carefully into the quinoa.

Risotto has the virtue of being a meal-in-one dish. Traditionally, it is made with Italian Arborio rice – a round variety that plumps up well as it absorbs liquid. However, as white rice – a carbohydrate converting more quickly to sugar – it's not ideal for those with diabetes. Pearl barley, which has a delicious nuttiness while modestly hosting, in this case, mushrooms and leeks, is an acceptable substitute. This is adapted from an original recipe by Emma Booth, who won a prize with it in *Stylist* magazine. Dried mushrooms aren't always easy to find but they serve as a taste engine, adding depth to the dish.

Pearl Barley 'Risotto' with Leeks and Mushrooms

SERVES 2–3

30g/1oz dried mushrooms (or replace with 200ml/7 fl oz warm water if unavailable)
2 garlic heads, cloves separated but skin left on
4 tbsp olive oil
200g/7oz fresh mushrooms, sliced thin
1½ leeks, finely chopped
2 tbsp white wine
200g/7oz pearl barley, rinsed thoroughly until the water runs clear
1 tsp fresh thyme, chopped
600ml/1 pint stock
50g/2oz Parmesan cheese, grated
black pepper and salt
a handful of chopped parsley (optional)

1 Put the dried mushrooms in a bowl and pour over 200ml/7 fl oz hot water. Leave to soften for 20 minutes. Strain into a bowl, reserving the liquid. Chop the softened mushrooms ready for use.

2 Preheat the oven to 190°C/375°F/Gas Mark 5. Put the garlic cloves in a bowl and mix with a tablespoon of olive oil. Empty them onto a shallow oven tray. Bake for about 15–20 minutes until they are soft, then set aside to cool.

3 Peel the garlic cloves and fork them into a mush. This is a messy business but it ends with a satisfying licking of the fingers.

4 Heat 2 tablespoons of oil in a pan and sauté the fresh mushrooms until they start to colour (this happens after they have released their moisture), then set aside.

5 Heat the last tablespoon of oil in a medium casserole (the one in which you will serve the risotto) and sauté the leeks over a medium heat until they soften and colour a little. Add the wine and let it evaporate, stirring continuously. Mix in the pearl barley, thyme and cooked garlic mush.

6 Have the stock in a pan close by, simmering on a low heat. Add the stock a ladleful at a time, stirring often, taking care the mix doesn't catch the bottom of the pan and burn. When there is none remaining, follow with the mushroom water (if you are using dried mushrooms) or warm water (if not).

7 When the barley is soft but still has a little bite in the centre (this took about 20 minutes for me), the risotto is ready for the dry and fresh mushrooms. Add them and stir in, followed by the Parmesan cheese. Season with black pepper and salt. Meredith recommends a sprinkling of parsley at the finish.

This recipe takes a little time, but when you come to cook it, the Zen of making risotto kicks in and it becomes a quiet meditation followed by a satisfying chew.

Desserts

I don't eat desserts. Well, that's not the whole
truth – Meredith sometimes makes a dessert for company
that's so good not to try it would be churlish. But I've never had
a craving for large portions of exotic 'afters'. For others, with
a sweet tooth, it's a sacrifice to forgo the third course and it's
true a good meal needs a grace note at the end to round it off;
a contrast to the savoury tastes of the main dish and something
that complements the coffee or tea to come.

I've been on the lookout for simple seasonal ways to finish a
meal. Fresh fruit served, uncooked, is a great standby for us
– apples and pears in winter; berries, peaches and apricots in
summer. These can be eaten simply as individual pieces or cut
up in a variety of fruit salads. Pomegranate seeds add colour,
texture and fun; yogurt and cinnamon often feature *chez
nous*. My favourite dessert, not always available, is a beautiful
ripe pear and a small piece of pecorino cheese. For everyday,
surprisingly, it's a piece of chocolate, with a high proportion
of cacao (90 per cent!), now regarded as a healthy choice.
One square with a small cup of black coffee is the perfect end
to lunch – that, a dried fig and a couple of dried apricots.
Here are some other ideas I found.

These showed up regularly at home in the 1950s. Large green cooking apples were always sitting around. I remember liking the puffiness of the apple flesh as it came out of the oven, scraping it away from the skin and mixing it with the syrupy sauce. My mother used golden syrup instead of honey.

Baked Apples

SERVES 4
4 large apples
a handful of raisins
zest of 1 lemon, chopped
a handful of walnut kernels, chopped
4 tbsp runny honey
4 cloves
100ml/4 fl oz water
yogurt, to serve

1 Preheat the oven to 180°C/350°F/Gas Mark 4.

2 Core the apples but leave them whole. Arrange them on an oven tray.

3 Put some raisins, a pinch of lemon zest, a few walnut pieces, a tablespoon of honey and a clove in each cavity. Pour the water into the tray. Bake for an hour, then remove and leave to cool before serving. A dollop of yogurt would meld well with the juices.

Our friend Romaine Hart brought this idea back from Los Angeles and passed it on. The three distinct flavours live happily together.

Fresh Strawberries with Lime Zest and Mint

SERVES 4
500g/1lb strawberries, halved
zest and juice of 2 limes
a handful of mint leaves, chopped small

1 Arrange the strawberries in a glass bowl (for preference). Sprinkle over the zest and the juice of the lime. Scatter over the chopped mint leaves.

Fresh fruit served,
uncooked, is a
seasonal standby for
us – apples and pears
in winter; berries,
peaches and apricots
in summer.

This is an everyday Mediterranean dessert – to which you can add fresh berries in season. Our single beehive in the garden provides a honey harvest two or three times a year. Each has a different taste depending on which plant's flower is being 'sucked' by the bees.

Greek Yogurt and Honey with Pan-roasted Walnuts

SERVES 4

a handful of walnut kernels, carefully dry-roasted on a low heat and broken up
4 x 125g/4oz pots Greek yogurt, strained through a sieve for 30 minutes to thicken
4 handfuls fresh berries (optional)
4 tsp honey

1 Scatter the walnuts over the yogurt and add the berries, if using.

2 Drizzle a little honey over the top. Delicious!

This is a simple, but fresh and delicious dessert to which you can add seasonal berries, such as strawberries, raspberries, blueberries or blackberries.

Mango, Peach and Pomegranate Seed Fruit Salad (with added berries, if available)

SERVES 4

1 ripe mango, peeled and stone removed
2 peaches (I favour the white), peeled and stones removed
handfuls each of berries in season
2 x 125g/4oz pots Greek yogurt, to serve
cinnamon, to serve

1 Slice the mango and peaches and assemble, together with any other chosen fruit, in a serving bowl or in individual bowls.

2 Serve with a dollop – lovely word! – of yogurt and a sprinkling of cinnamon. You will of course need to vary the amount of fruit according to how many people you are serving.

This recipe is adapted from a recipe in Diana Henry's *Food from Plenty*.

Baked Apricots, Honey and Fresh Orange Juice

SERVES 3–4
120ml/4 fl oz fresh orange juice
1 tbsp lemon juice
20 ripe apricots, halved and
   stones removed
seeds from 5 cardamom pods, crushed
2–3 tbsp runny honey
Greek yogurt, to serve

1 Preheat the oven to 180°C/350°F/Gas Mark 4.

2 Pour the orange and lemon juice into a shallow ovenproof dish.

3 Arrange the apricots, cut sides up, in a single layer in the dish.

4 Sprinkle over the cardamom seeds and drizzle over the honey.

5 Bake for about 20–25 minutes, depending on the size of the apricots. They need to be soft. Remove and serve – a dollop of Greek yogurt always goes well.

This classic Moroccan dessert works well after a rich main course. If you can find blood oranges, they make a good show.

Moroccan Orange Salad

SERVES 4
4 oranges, peeled, pithed and
   sliced thin
2 tbsp orange blossom water
a few mint leaves, chopped
4 untreated apricots, chopped
a sprinkling of cinnamon

1 Arrange the orange slices in a glass or white bowl. Sprinkle over the orange blossom water.

2 Scatter over the mint and apricots, and a shake of cinnamon. Refrigerate until the start of the meal.

Our friend Lina's dessert is sumptuous and rich. A tablespoon with some yogurt is enough to finish off a meal.

Lina's Dried Fruit Compôte

SERVES 10

1.2l/2 pints water
2 rosehip teabags
425g/14oz prunes
250g/8oz dried apricots
375g/12oz dried figs
50g/2oz raisins
30g/1oz dried cranberries or goji berries(optional if difficult to find)
5 cloves
1 cinnamon stick
50g/2oz flaked almonds or toasted pine nuts, to serve
yogurt or crème fraîche, to serve

1 Boil the water, pour over the teabags in a china bowl and leave for at least 10 minutes to steep.

2 Discard the teabags and pour the liquid into a pan. Add the dried fruit and spices, and simmer for 15 minutes – until enough water is boiled off to leave a syrup on the fruit.

3 Leave to cool. Serve with the flaked almonds or toasted pine nuts sprinkled over and yogurt or crème fraîche.

Sundries

‘Breakfast is the most important meal of the day.’ – I'm sure my mother said that a few times! Breakfast before I set off on my walk this morning was the same as every morning! Dull? Not for me – I look forward to it! Maybe we are at our most conservative, most in need of ritual just after waking up, but I find the assembling and eating of this bowl of goodies a daily delight.

Breakfast

‘All happiness depends on a leisurely breakfast.’

John Gunther

‘Only dull people are brilliant at breakfast.’

Oscar Wilde

SERVES 1

large organic oat flakes

freshly cracked walnuts – watch out for rogue pieces of shell that can crack your teeth

1 dried apricot, chopped

1 cooked prune

½ x 125g/4oz pot of organic yogurt

oat/almond milk, unsweetened, enough to moisten

ground cinnamon, to sprinkle

TO FOLLOW

2 slices 100 per cent rye bread, toasted with a little butter and pear and apple fruit spread (no added sugar)

1 Assemble in the order above in your favourite breakfast bowl, ending with a sprinkle of cinnamon.

2 Follow with the rye toast.

MEREDITH'S VERSION OF BREAKFAST HEAVEN
Porridge

Cooked oats, large and small flakes, milk, organic yogurt, a cooked prune, seasonal fruit, cinnamon sprinkled over.

Vinaigrettes and Sauces for Dressing

EVERYDAY VINAIGRETTE

A classic French dressing.

1 garlic clove, peeled and pulped in a mortar
with a pinch of salt

1 tbsp balsamic vinegar

1 tsp Dijon mustard

5 tbsp olive oil

1 Mix together the first three ingredients thoroughly.

2 Add the olive oil and whisk to a viscous delight.

Or try this alternative, without mustard:

3 tbsp olive oil

1 tbsp balsamic vinegar

juice of ½ lemon

salt

OLIVE OIL AND LEMON JUICE VINAIGRETTE

A delicate sauce.

a pinch of salt

½ tsp Dijon mustard

juice of ½ lemon

3–4 tbsp olive oil

1 Mix the salt with the mustard and then the lemon juice.

2 Add the olive oil and whisk.

SALAD DRESSING WITH ANCHOVIES

A bold vinaigrette.

4 anchovy fillets, chopped

1 garlic clove, peeled and pulped with a little salt in a mortar

a turn of the pepper mill

2 tbsp red wine vinegar

4 tbsp olive oil

salt to taste, remembering the anchovies are salty

1 Add the chopped anchovy fillets to the garlic pulp in a mortar and meld them into a loose paste.

2 Add a little pepper, mix in the vinegar, then whisk in the oil.

3 Taste for salt and add extra if needed.

MAYONNAISE-LIKE DRESSING

Not as soft and unctuous as mayonnaise, of course, but good with salmon, for instance, and asparagus – and it does not involve the irksome though rewarding business of making mayonnaise!
Heresy, I know . . .

1 tbsp cider vinegar

1 tsp Dijon mustard

juice of ¼ lemon

4–5 tbsp extra-virgin olive

1 Whisk the cider vinegar, mustard and lemon juice together.

2 As you would when making a mayonnaise, add the oil slowly, whisking it in as you go.

SAUCE FOR ASPARAGUS AND ARTICHOKES

This recipe, based on one by Geraldene Holt, is a tasty change from the more traditional vinaigrettes to accompany welcome spring arrivals.

SERVES 4

salt and pepper

1 tsp Dijon mustard

1 tsp white wine vinegar

4 tbsp olive oil

2 tbsp crème fraîche

1 Put a pinch of salt and pepper into a mixing bowl.

2 Mix in the mustard and vinegar.

3 Add the oil – stirring gently to emulsify.

4 Fold in the crème fraîche.

5 Taste for seasoning and adjust if necessary.

How to Make Garam Masala (Hot Spice Mix)

Garam masala may be an ingredient new to some. The 'hot', or garam, is not a spicy hot but rather a heat that warms the body (in principle). I learnt about this subtle and delicate mix from Kris Dhillon's *The Curry Secret*. She writes: '. . . the theory comes from the Hindu concept of medicine and diet called tridosha, which teaches that some foods have a warming effect on the body while others have a cooling effect. Spices such as cardamoms, cloves, cinnamon and nutmeg are garam constituents of this aromatic mixture.'

Garam masala is usually added towards the end of the cooking process. It can also be sprinkled over cooked food to enhance the flavour. A mixture of spices, it has infinite variations. You can buy it (just as you can buy curry powder) or you can easily and quickly make your own. This version is from the wonderful Indian actress and food writer Madhur Jaffrey, author of *Indian Cookery*.

1 tbsp cardamom seeds	5cm/2in cinnamon stick
1 tsp cumin seeds	1 tsp whole cloves
1 tsp black peppercorns	½ small nutmeg, grated

1 Whizz all the ingredients to a fine powder in a spice or coffee grinder.

How to Make *Labneh* (Yogurt Cheese)

Labneh is simply yogurt drained of its whey for several hours to produce a thick cheese-like consistency. Light flavourings can be added at the start.

SERVES 4

a cut square of muslin

a sieve

2 medium bowls

4 x 125g/4oz pots yogurt

seasonings of choice: ½ teaspoon salt, cumin powder, coriander powder, lemon zest, etc.

string

1 Spread the muslin over a sieve and press it down. Place the sieve over a medium bowl.

2 Pour the yogurt into a bowl and whisk it smooth. Add seasonings of choice at this stage.

3 Carefully spoon this mix into the muslin. Gather the square together, so the yogurt forms a ball. Twist the muslin in order to tie it and secure with string. You can help the process along with a gentle squeeze or just leave the yogurt ball to drip for a couple of hours into the bowl, preferably in the fridge. It will reduce surprisingly in volume – how much depends on how thick you want it. Try it a few times.

4 You could put the yogurt straight into the sieve and over a bowl into the fridge but this will take longer – 12 hours perhaps – as you obviously can't squeeze the liquid out.

How to Cook Dried Beans and Chickpeas (Garbanzo Beans)

I like a plate of beans, with olive oil swirled over them. There are good-quality beans available now in glass jars, which can be quickly heated up. But perhaps you have a packet of dry white beans that has spent some time on a shelf, daring you to do something with it. Ever present, silently reproachful, waiting for some action, they can be intimidating! The sooner they are treated, the better, and this way is simplest.

SERVES 1

250g/8oz dried beans

salt and pepper

½ organic vegetable stock cube

best olive oil, to serve

1 Put the beans in a bowl and cover them with cold water. Leave to soak overnight.

2 Preheat the oven to 160°C/325°F/Gas Mark 3. Drain the beans and rinse them. Put them in a medium casserole/pot/pan and cover them again by the top of a thumb joint of cold water. Cover the casserole and bring to the boil on the hob. Place it on the middle shelf of the oven and cook for 40 minutes.

3 Test for softness, leaving longer if necessary; the older the beans, the longer they will take. You can always add more hot water. Add a teaspoon of salt to the casserole and leave to cool in the liquid.

4 When you are ready to eat, reheat the beans in their liquid, adding half an organic vegetable stock cube, crumbled. Drain the beans and serve them hot. Season to taste with salt and pepper, adding a swirl of the best olive oil you have.

Home-Roasted Nuts

Healthier, tastier and cheaper than the bought variety, roasted nuts are also quick and easy to do. They are a conversation starter too.

250g/8oz raw cashews

1 tsp olive oil

sprinkling of fine salt

1 Preheat the oven to 180°C/350°F/Gas Mark 4.

2 Put the nuts in a bowl. Add the oil and turn and turn until all the nuts are coated. Sprinkle in some salt and turn again.

3 Cover a shallow baking tray with foil. Lay out the nuts in a single layer.

4 Roast for 10 minutes in the middle of the oven, then check for doneness: eat one, gingerly. They should be light golden – like the commercial ones! Cook a little longer if you need to.

5 Leave to cool off and try not to eat them all at one sitting.

RAW ALMONDS

Replace the cashews with raw almonds and follow the same method as above – they may need an extra 10 minutes' cooking time. Do check them, though – burnt nuts aren't nice!

Brown Basmati Rice

Brown basmati is my rice of choice. It is unrefined and tastes nuttily delicious. Everyone has their own way of cooking rice. This is my method of the moment, introduced to me by our friend Simone Sarti.

SERVES 4

250g/8oz basmati brown rice

½ tsp salt

bay leaf, if you have one to hand

1 Using a sieve, rinse the rice thoroughly. Rest the sieve holding the rice on the rim of a bowl filled with water. Soak the rice in the water for 20 minutes or longer.

2 Lift the sieve out of the water and empty the rice into a saucepan. Add enough water to top the rice by roughly 2.5cm/1in. Bring to the boil, add the salt and bay leaf, if using, and cover. Cook over the lowest heat possible – using a heat diffuser if you have one – for about 25 minutes, resisting the temptation to peek under the lid.

3 Check for doneness. Cook a little longer if necessary, then let it rest, covered, for 10 minutes.

A Less Tearful Way of Chopping Onions

Holding the onion pieces firmly together helps prevent the noxious fumes escaping. Be careful – keep the sticking plaster at hand for the first couple of tries!

1 Peel the onion.

2 Halve it from top to toe.

3 Lay one half flat with the root-end facing away from you. Starting at the right side and with the tip of a sharp knife, cut down just above the root. Then work your way over the dome to the left side with similar cuts.

4 Hold the half firmly with your left hand, swivel it, keeping it in shape, and with the knife in your right hand carefully cut into the onion low and horizontally. Do the same several times as you work your way over the dome.

5 Lastly, cut down the vertical – working from right to left and, *voilà*, you have a chopped onion!

Simple Herb Teas

We have a mad mint patch, which starts to show some time in late March and lasts through October. It is unstoppable and a great source for a great sauce (page 69).

● For an infusion of mint tea, all you need is a couple of leaves in a cup or pot with boiling water poured over.

● Leave it to infuse for a minute or so and you have a wonderfully fresh-tasting drink. You can do the same with thyme, rosemary and sage; root ginger too – so much nicer than a teabag!

The GI and the GL

The Glycaemic Index (GI) is a measure, on the scale of 1 to 100, ranking carbohydrates according to their effect on our blood glucose levels and thus their post-meal impact.

The Glycaemic Load (GL) is a measure of the impact of the glucose in a single *portion* of food.

The GI Foundation neatly sums it up thus: *'Not all carbohydrate foods are created equal, in fact they behave quite differently in our bodies. The glycaemic index or GI describes this difference by ranking carbohydrates according to their effect on our blood glucose levels. Choosing low GI carbs – the ones that produce only small fluctuations in our blood glucose and insulin levels – is the secret to long-term health, reducing your risk of heart disease and diabetes and is the key to sustainable weight loss.'*

LIQUID CONVERSIONS

IMPERIAL	METRIC	AMERICAN
½ fl oz	15 ml	1 tablespoon
1 fl oz	30 ml	⅛ cup
2 fl oz	60 ml	¼ cup
4 fl oz	120 ml	½ cup
8 fl oz	240 ml	1 cup
16 fl oz	480 ml	1 pint

In British, Australian and often Canadian recipes an imperial pint is 20 fl oz. American recipes use the American pint measurement, which is 16 fl oz.

Index